PRISONER
OF WAR
Der Luftwaffe

PRISONER OF WAR
Der Luftwaffe

Frank Farnsley

PENTLAND PRESS, INC.

ENGLAND · USA · SCOTLAND

PUBLISHED BY PENTLAND PRESS, INC.
5124 Bur Oak Circle, Raleigh, North Carolina 27612
United States of America
919-782-0281

ISBN 1-57197-031-2
Library of Congress Catalog Card Number 96-69082

Printed in the United States of America

Dedication

This book is dedicated to 1st Lt. Vernon Huff, our bombardier, and TSgt. Nicholas Kish, our nose gunner, who were killed on our last mission. Also it's dedicated to the memory of TSgt. Ralph Gage from Vienna, Illinois, a very good friend who lost his life on a mission while flying as a ball turret gunner from England. For his wife, Eleen, and his daughter, Dianne, this book is also dedicated to my dear, departed, lifelong friend, Marvin Alford. And of course it's dedicated to the other members of my crew. Special recognition goes to 1st Lt. Paul Stillions, our copilot, who assisted me in gathering information concerning our crew members. Also special recognition goes to my wife, Clara, and my son, Kevin, whose encouragement helped inspire me to write this book.

As our crew ambled happily toward our plane, the American Maid, the silhouettes of our B-24 bombers were reflecting the first glimmer of morning sunlight. It was 26 June 1944, another exciting day for us. We were Lt. David Himes's crew, and our nose gunner, Jim Catron from West Virginia, who had completed his fiftieth mission the day before, walked with us. We chatted excitedly about celebrating because Jim had finished his missions, and today, Lou Staudenemier, our ball turret gunner from Pennsylvania, and Herman "Herky" Strietburger, our radio operator from New York, were each finishing their fiftieth mission. We had flown five consecutive missions, the last being in Ploesti, Romania, in the oil fields which supplied Germany with much of its oil. Tomorrow was our day off. Our party to celebrate had been planned; for the last month Ellis Covan, our tail gunner from Alabama, and I had saved most of our double shots

T/Sgt. Louis Staudinemier, 1943

of whiskey we were given for soothing our nerves after we returned from our missions and were being debriefed. We were all happier than usual; the rest of us had only a few missions left before we finished our tour. We all had visions of our return to the States and our homes for a long furlough.

As the top turret and armor gunner, it was my duty to check the guns, bomb load, and to see that each crew member had a parachute. This I did quite methodically as I had done many times before. It was different today. I was thinking of returning to Florence, Mississippi, and our home on a farm just a few miles away. Our pilot, Lt. David Himes from Oklahoma, seemed a bit

more excited than usual. He was twenty-seven years old, and to us he seemed older because he was the most serious and most "military" of us all. He was a no-nonsense guy who reprimanded us for talking on the intercom, especially Ellis and me, when we were at high altitude. Our new nose gunner, Nick Kish from Pennsylvania, had replaced Jim Catron who had finished his missions the day before when we had bombed and severely damaged the Ploesti oil fields in Romania. I talked to Jim briefly as I made my bomb and gun inspection

Herman Strietburger, Radio Operator, 1943

tour of our plane. When I walked by the waist gunner, radio operator Herman Strietburger from Manhattan, New York, he assured me his guns were okay. Herky liked the waist gun position best of all. Ordinarily he would have flown my top turret position, but he had traded the top turret to me for my waist position, which made us both happy. Lou, our ball turret gunner, said that Herky liked the waist gun position because it offered the quickest exit in case we had to bail out. Lou had a witty sense of humor and spoke with an Irish accent although he was of German descent. He had grown up in an Irish neighborhood. Lou had instructed Herky that it was his duty to see that his ball turret had been successfully raised in case of an emergency bail-out because the turret sometimes became stuck in the lowered position and a waist gunner had to raise it manually. Ellis Covan, our six-foot tall tail gunner who claimed he had plenty of room in his turret, which we didn't believe, shouted at me, "For God's sake, Frank, don't use the relief tube today. Remember two days ago you pissed all over my turret—it froze, and I couldn't see a damned thing!"

I assured him I'd try not to and that I had only used the relief tube once during all of our missions. Ellis was my best friend on our crew. He was a big, handsome boy from Alabama. He and I often went into Lecce, Italy, only fourteen miles from our Ninety-eighth Bomb Group's base which was located in the heel of the boot of southern Italy. Ellis was my protector as well as my friend. I could be quite sassy with the guys in arguments because no one dared to lay a hand on me while Ellis was there, and I never got sassy with anyone unless he was present.

Eugene Bailey from Savannah, Georgia, was our other waist gunner. Gene had a broad southern accent, different from my thick Mississippi one. He would say, "Put oout your cigarette," for example. "Oout" rhymed with toot. Gene had a good sense of humor and was very friendly.

Back on the flight deck I chatted briefly with Paul Stillions, our copilot, from Illinois. Paul was the most handsome of us all. Actually we thought he was the best-looking man in the Ninety-eighth Bomb Group. He was also a calm, friendly, and very considerate person and was probably the best liked by the rest of us.

Our bombardier, Vernon Huff from Texas, was the smallest one on our crew. He was only about five feet four inches tall, friendly, and calm. As he went to his position in the nose of our plane, Bob Moore, our navigator, remarked to me what a beautiful day it was; there was not a cloud in the blue Italian sky. Bob was from Minneapolis, Minnesota. He had a dark complexion, and was a good-looking young man. He was good-natured and had a ready smile for all.

Robert Moore, Navigator, 1945

Several days earlier, Ellis and I had gone into Lecce, Italy, on a pass. Ellis had borrowed our first sergeant's jeep. Previously Ellis had rescued the first sergeant in a brawl and the sergeant was appreciative enough to lend Ellis his jeep. Ellis and I had drunk too much Italian wine and were still "high" when we went to the mess hall. We were not aware that General Twining, our Fifteenth Air Force commander, was on the base for an inspection tour. As Ellis and I stood in the mess line, we were both loud and boisterous. Previously, because of my arrogance and bravery while Ellis was there to protect me, I had been nicknamed "the Rebel" because I could do a rather good Civil War-type imitation of a rebel yell. Suddenly I banged my mess kit on the wall and emitted two loud rebel yells. Almost immediately the general appeared.

"What's the matter, son? Don't you feel well?" he asked.

"I feel fine. What about you?" I replied.

He only smiled, patted me on my back, and walked away. Later Lou, who was standing next to me, told me that he had expected the general to rip off my sergeant's stripes. But the general was obviously quite understanding.

At about 5 A.M. the American Maid, along with thirty-four other B-24 bombers in our 343d Squadron, made a successful take-off. Our target for today was a Messerschmidt aircraft factory on the outskirts of Vienna, Austria.

We all settled into our positions because it wouldn't take long to cross the Adriatic Sea and reach high altitude.

Lieutenant Himes talked to each of us over the intercom to make sure it was working and to know that each of us was in position. For a short while Ellis, the tail gunner, and I talked about finishing our missions and going back to the States together; we each were on our thirty-eighth mission and knew we'd finish our fiftieth in about two weeks.

Time passed slowly as we flew over the mountains of Yugoslavia. The scenery was beautiful; the cloudless blue sky gave us a striking panoramic view of the mountains.

"Look, see the planes? They're our P-51 escorts!" shouted Ellis, the tail gunner, over the intercom. "That son of a bitch is shooting at us!" Ellis screamed.

We shifted from slow motion to breakneck speed. German ME-109s were attacking from several directions. Hundreds of caliber-fifty machine gun fire filled the air as gunners from our formation of thirty-five planes opened fire on the ME-109s. In a matter of minutes the enemy planes turned tail and disappeared as suddenly as they'd arrived. Gradually we calmed down. We were slowing down again. Now there was only flack. We returned to our nerve-racking, slow-motion pace. Once again we were praying to be spared from these devilish black puffs of smoke as each minute seemed to last an hour long. We made a sharp right turn. I knew we were near the target and were making our bomb run. It was my first mission in which we were the lead plane of our squadron. This made all of us more confident—we had never seen a lead plane go down. The flack seemed even thicker. Now we not only felt the concussions of exploding ammunition, but we could hear what sounded like someone throwing gravel against our plane. This noise was fragments of exploding shells.

Suddenly our plane heaved and lurched violently to the right. I swung the top turret around. Our number one engine had taken a direct hit. It was knocked out. Then smoke poured from our number two engine, and its propeller came to a stop. Lieutenant Himes had feathered it. (Feathering means fixing the propeller blades so they will not turn; this is done to preserve power.) Our plane slowed down and leaned heavily to the right. We were losing altitude and falling out of formation. Then I could see the tail gunner in the last plane of our formation waving good-bye to us. My heart pounded as I thought, We've got to bail out.

Before I could react a German ME-109 made a pass, firing at us. I let go with a dozen or so bursts of gunfire. The tracer ammunition showed that I was getting direct hits. Why doesn't it go down? I thought. I could see smoke coming from the ME-109 as it dived below us. Now it seemed that all hell had broken loose. At least four ME-109s were attacking us. I hadn't realized that six of our ten caliber-fifty machine guns had been knocked out. Too busy to think of being scared, I fired as rapidly as I could at the ever-oncoming German planes. My guns stopped firing – my ammunition was gone. As I swung my turret around I could see a huge hole in the fuselage of our plane between me and Lou, the ball turret gunner. I felt panic almost overtake me as I dropped from my turret, ripping loose my headset and oxygen mask. I grabbed my chest-pack parachute and fastened it to my chute harness. Then I struggled with the bomb bay door handle; it wouldn't budge. Flames were pouring from the cracks in the bomb bay. We were on fire, and luckily the doors hadn't opened. After I scrambled along the catwalk to the nose of the plane, Bob, our navigator, Huff, our bombardier, and Nick, our nose gunner, had opened one half of the nose-wheel door. I grabbed the other half of the door and opened it.

"Jump, Frank!" yelled Bob.

"Go ahead!" I screamed. "You were here first!"

"Damn it, Frank, jump!" Bob shouted.

I jumped, feet first, and counted, "One, two, three," then pulled my rip cord. I felt a strong jolt as my chute opened. I was only a few feet below our falling plane. We were told to count to ten before pulling our chute cord. I could have been caught on the falling plane, I thought, and I was quite relieved as I plunged downward. Suddenly I was conscious of praying aloud. I wasn't thinking of praying; the words just flowed from my mouth. I could hear myself asking for forgiveness for everything I'd done wrong, and as I did so I thought of my family back home, as most of my transgressions centered around my family and the misdeeds I'd done there. A comforting calmness engulfed me, and my fear and panic left. I knew I was going to survive and be safe. Also I felt a presence; not a person, but a presence of comfort surrounding me. I was no longer afraid. I could see open farmland below, and in the direction I was falling there was a river lined with trees. Maybe I could sail across the river and take cover in the trees. We couldn't be too far from Yugoslavia; the partisans there would help us escape. We'd been told about them, I recalled. Then I saw several people running on the ground. As I descended further I could see one of our crew being chased by two people. I saw a German fighter plane coming in my direction – it was an ME-109. As the plane got closer I remembered hearing that flyers who'd bailed out had been shot and killed by German fighter planes as they were falling. The plane turned and flew lower as if it were going to land. My heart was pounding, but I felt relieved. Just before I hit the ground I could see three farm workers with hoes and other farm tools running in my direction. Also about three hundred yards ahead I saw two soldiers coming toward me. I threw myself back as I landed; my head was jolted. I realized I still was wearing my steel helmet. Frantically I unfastened my chute harness and ran toward the oncoming German soldiers. The three farmers were just a short distance behind me. Later I thought I had set a new track record as I raced toward the soldiers and threw my arms up and surrendered to them. The two soldiers marched me across the field.

"Austria?" I asked them.

"Ungarn, Ungarn," one of them replied.

Then I knew we had crossed the border from Austria and were in Hungary. As we approached a nearby village about a dozen civilians came toward us. An old man with a full white beard looked at me and shouted, "Al Capone! Chicago! Luft gangsters! You come to kill our women and children! You drop toys filled with dynamite and poison lollipops!"

One of the German soldiers pushed the old man aside. Soon we were in an open courtyard. There, in this small Hungarian village, stood Lieutenant Himes, our pilot, Lieutenant Moore, our navigator, and Lieutenant Stillions, our copilot. Lieutenant Stillions had a bloody gash on his forehead and was standing on one leg. Tears flowed from my eyes as I said, "Paul, you've hurt your leg?"

"I think my ankle's broken," he replied.

The six German soldiers soon left. A Hungarian soldier was left to guard us. It was soon obvious that the Hungarian guard spoke no English, but he made no objection as we talked softly to each other. We all seemed to be in shock or a daze as we sat near each other on the ground. About ten minutes later Hungarian civilians who had been watching from a short distance came closer. One, a pretty, young, dark-haired girl who looked to be about sixteen or seventeen, came closer to us.

"What is it like in America?" she asked. "Are all the people wealthy?"

At first no one answered. We were surprised that she seemed to be so friendly.

"Not really," I said. "I know a lot of poor people back there."

"Frank, don't talk to her! Keep quiet. All we can tell these people is our name, rank, and our serial number," Lieutenant Himes said rather sternly.

"I was in England going to school and came home on vacation. Then the war began," said the young girl. "I'm a Jew, but we have many friends. The Hungarian soldiers don't bother us."

Several years later when I read the book The Diary of Ann Frank I realized that this girl had a close resemblance to Ann. I wondered if she had ended up in a concentration camp and whether she had survived the war.

A few minutes later a cart pulled by two oxen and driven by a Hungarian civilian appeared. The four of us were escorted into the small, two-wheeled cart and the Hungarian soldier with his rifle had to stand. There wasn't enough room to sit down. Paul, our copilot, braced himself on my shoulder because his broken ankle was hurting. The oxen plodded slowly along a dirt and gravel road, switching their tails to brush away the annoying flies.

About two hours later we arrived in a larger village. The local church bell was chiming; it was noon. Once again we were taken to an open courtyard. This time it was surrounded by a brick wall about six feet tall. Already standing by the wall were Ellis, our tail gunner, Herky, our radio operator, Lou, our ball turret gunner, and Gene, our waist gunner. As we had landed by parachute we were scattered miles apart. Now they had captured eight of our crew of eleven. We wondered about Vern, our bombardier, and Nick, our nose gunner. Shortly afterward we found out that Nick had not jumped and had gone down with the plane. Then a German soldier showed us a bloody life jacket, a "Mae West," we called them. We tried to hold back tears as we realized that Vernon Huff, our bombardier, had been killed by the Hungarian civilians who would have killed us all if the German soldiers had not rescued us. We were now lined up around the brick wall.

"Are they going to shoot us now?" Ellis said in a high-pitched, nervous voice.

"Shut up, don't give them any ideas," I whispered in a voice just as nervous as his.

We were all tired, hungry, and thirsty; so far we had not had either food or water. I needed to go to the bathroom. I asked one of the German soldiers. He led me into a nearby building. Outside the bathroom on the wall was a large map of Europe. I paused and pointed to the spot in Hungary where I thought we were.

"Nein," replied the guard as he pointed to our location on the map.

Much to my dismay we appeared to be only ten to fifteen miles from the Yugoslavian border. Finally we were given water; it was the best I'd ever drunk.

At about 2 P.M. Monday 26 June 1944 the eight of us survivors were marched to a Hungarian railroad station and put on a train. In about a half hour we arrived in Zambathley, Hungary. We were taken to an old jail-like red brick building. In this building we were joined by ten members of other crews who had been captured. Our German guards turned us over to Hungarian guards who took us into a large room with no windows. Inside the room there were about a dozen wooden platforms that resembled beds. Being thoroughly exhausted we immediately collapsed on them. Instantly several Hungarian guards yelled at us, and with fixed bayonets pointed at us they made us understand that we were to stack the beds in one corner of the room. After we had done this, the guards lined us up facing the walls around the room. They wouldn't let us touch the walls and indicated that we were to stand at attention. When everyone was quiet I noticed a large wall clock and could hear the ticking; it was three-thirty in the afternoon. Except for sighing and occasional loud breathing, there wasn't a sound except the ticking of the clock.

About an hour later, Ellis said, "I can't stand up any longer," and he proceeded to sit on the floor. A guard rushed toward him with his bayonet and stuck him in his thigh. Ellis jumped up and stood like the rest of us. Every four hours the guards changed. Each time a new guard came on duty he would walk by us and grab about every other one of us, slapping and punching each one he'd grabbed. This procedure continued all through the night. The only relief we got was when the guard would allow us to go relieve ourselves in the corner of the room. The guard would allow us about two minutes and then would order us out. At least we could sit and rest a bit. So every four hours, one by one, we'd all ask to go to the rest room to get a couple of minutes of precious rest. All through the night and next day the beatings and rest room procedure continued with the changing of the guards. Finally at 3:30 P.M. two German officers came in and told us we could sit down. Having stood for twenty-four hours we were completely exhausted and collapsed onto the floor. Then we were given bread and jam and water. To me this was the very best food I'd ever eaten; it had been at least thirty-four hours since breakfast at about 5 A.M. on 26 June.

About an hour later we were marched a few blocks to the nearby train station in Zambathley, Hungary. We were soon on a crowded passenger train, destination unknown. Four armed German guards were assigned to us twenty American airmen. As our train speeded along through the Hungarian countryside, I realized that, against army regulations, I had my wallet in my pants pocket. So far the Germans and Hungarians had not searched us except for a superficial search for concealed weapons, and much to my surprise they had not taken my wallet. In my wallet was a pass to go into Lecce, Italy, and a few Italian lira, about five dollar's worth. I wondered how I could get rid of my wallet and its contents, because a German guard was seated directly across from me. I was also ashamed and afraid of what my crew members would think of me being so careless. I was concerned because this might cause trouble and extra interrogation for all of us. When the German guard across the aisle from me dozed off to sleep, I slowly withdrew my wallet from my pocket and began tearing the pass and Italian money into bits. With a little saliva I rolled the bits into small pills. Being afraid to throw the bits onto the floor because the guard could see them, I stuck them into my shoes, hoping to be able to dispose of them later. I left my wallet there, empty except for a picture of a girlfriend back in Mississippi. It was a picture of Wilma Harper, the valedictorian of my 1940 graduation class from Florence High

School. Wilma was a brilliant girl, very pretty, with a charming personality. I was hoping that she'd not get serious with anyone else before I returned to the States. Over a year later when I finally got back to Florence, Mississippi, I learned she was engaged to an American airman who had finished his missions while flying as a gunner on a bomber in England. But her picture, which the Germans allowed me to keep, gave me much comfort while I was a POW. Among the twenty-four of us, I was the only POW who had a picture of his girlfriend.

Near midnight of 27 June 1944 our train pulled into Budapest, Hungary. We were quickly put into a van, or "drummer's truck" as we called them back in 1944, and were taken to an old four-story red brick jail. After we entered a large room on the first floor, we were strip-searched. We had to remove all of our clothes, even our shoes and socks. Then, one by one, each of us had to bend over and spread our "cheeks."

"Are they checking us for piles?" asked Ellis, the tail gunner.

Actually they were checking us for rectal compasses which somehow they knew we'd been given. The Germans found nothing but cloth maps of the region of Europe over which we'd flown. Each of us had one. When the German searchers shook my shoes, all the little paper pills I'd made of my pass to Lecce, Italy, and the Italian money fell to the floor. One German picked them up and tried to unroll them, but since they'd been chewed and mixed with saliva, it was to no avail. The German threw the pills into a small box. This incident made the Germans suspicious of me. I was immediately taken to the fourth floor of the jail and shoved into a small cell which was about eight by ten feet.

The furniture in my cell consisted of a small iron-framed cot which had a straw mattress, two wool blankets, and a pillow. Also there was a five-gallon bucket in one corner of the cell which was my private toilet. The four-inch-thick door had a peephole through which a guard peeked about every four hours. I could tell when I was being observed because I could hear a slight noise each time he pushed its cover aside. Being completely exhausted, I went to bed. I didn't hear a sound until daylight, at about six o'clock the next morning.

My cell door suddenly opened and a Hungarian orderly came in carrying a small aluminum bowl of broth with a few bread crumbs floating on the top. Also I was given a small round loaf of rye bread about four inches in diameter. I ate the broth and bread. Being wide awake my thoughts wandered to my other seven crew members who were also in this antique jail. Were they in solitary confinement like I, or were they two or more together in a cell?

As I glanced around the room I noticed dates written on the walls. These dates ranged from 1944 as far back as 1753. Having been an avid reader and a lover of poetry, Tennyson's line "Stone walls do not a prison make" flashed through my mind. Not true; pure propaganda, I thought. I tried to go back to sleep but couldn't. If only I had someone to talk to, I thought. I walked to my small cell window and stared at the view. My cell was in the front of the jail and two people, probably jail personnel, walked up the front sidewalk and into the jail. To the left, about thirty feet from the jail, an apricot tree about ten feet tall was full of fruit just beginning to ripen. Did those apricots look good! In a few days they would be juicy and ripe. A church bell in a nearby church began to peal. I counted seven rings and knew it was 7 A.M. Again my thoughts rambled. Had my parents and my three brothers and four sisters been notified that I'd been shot down and was missing in action? I could see Mom crying as she read the telegram and Dad struggling to hold back tears. I'd never seen Dad actually cry, but I had seen a few tears run down his cheeks at my four-year-old brother's funeral. Little Clyde had been accidentally killed by a shotgun blast on Thanksgiving Day in 1931. I was nine years old at the time. It was my first funeral to attend, and I had witnessed the accident. I'd asked Mom a few minutes after his death, "Is Clyde plumb dead, Mom?" I couldn't understand death and didn't comprehend its finality. Dad also had moist cheeks in May of 1943 at my twenty-four-year-old sister's funeral; Wilma had died quite unexpectedly of an epileptic seizure which made my unexpected furlough back home quite traumatic.

Then I began to face reality. I must not feel sorry for myself. I wanted to survive, and I knew self-pity wouldn't help. I was getting bored as well. I couldn't sleep as I lay on my bunk. Then I noticed that the orderly had left the aluminum spoon when he took my empty bowl. I took the spoon and inscribed "June 28, 1944" on the wall near some other dates written many years ago. I noticed writing which I couldn't read. It must be Hungarian, I decided. I took the spoon and began to scratch on the wall, "Stone walls do not a prison make, nor iron bars a cage."

I stopped abruptly, thought for a few seconds, then wrote below it, "Bah Humbug!"

Then I began to write poems I'd memorized in school. Because I had fear of the guards seeing the freshly scratched writing on the wall, I wrote on the part of the wall that wouldn't be noticed when the door was open. For almost nineteen days I spent my time inscribing most of the poetry I'd memorized on the wall with the spoon handle. I covered a wide range, from "Little Boy Blue" to Shakespeare's "Friends, Romans, and countrymen, lend me your ears."

Along with looking out my cell window and watching shot-down American flyers who'd been captured being brought into the jail, usually five to ten of them a day, this was the way I kept from brooding too much. But I'd never been so lonesome; solitary confinement was the worst part of my captivity. I also made a mark on the wall each day so I could keep track of the date. On the evening of my fifth day at about midnight, my door opened and a guard ushered a shot-down American airman into my cell. A straw mattress was thrown onto the floor, and the guard left. I was elated to have company. Lieutenant James Kovach, my cell mate, was the navigator of a B-24 crew from another base in Italy. After talking for about ten minutes we went to sleep. At about 7 A.M. our cell door opened and a guard called and motioned for me to follow him. I was taken to the first floor of the jail and into a large room where about a dozen captured American flyers were eating bread and jam and drinking coffee. After a few minutes of eating the delicious meal, I talked with a captured copilot and learned that all of them were officers on crews that had been shot down the day before. Then it occurred to me that since these officers were being fed so well, and I'd been starving on the small loaf of bread and cup of broth each day, why not take the place of the navigator whom the guard had left in my cell? Obviously the guard had us mixed up. After we'd eaten all the bread and jam, a German officer gave orders for us to line up as he called out our names. I'll get in line when he calls James Kovach, I thought, and hope the rest of these guys keep their mouths shut.

After about ten names had been called, the officer said, "James Kovach." No one answered for a few seconds. Then I said, "Here," as I got at the end of the line.

Immediately one of the American captives said, "He's not James Kovach. James Kovach is on my crew."

The German officer pushed me toward the door. He roughed me up as he shouted orders for the guard to take me back to my cell. Soon I was pushed into my cell, and James Kovach was taken down to join his crew. I felt darned good. I'd eaten the bread and jam and felt more content than I'd been since we were captured. Then it dawned on me. What if I'd taken James Kovach's place, name and all? My family would never have known that I was a POW. Then, after a year, I'd be declared dead. I was glad it didn't happen because of the grief my family would have gone through.

A few days later as I was eating my daily bowl of soup, I noticed a name and message had been scratched on my aluminum bowl. It said, "Help! Help! I'm Bob Hedrick. I've been here thirty-seven days and I'm starving!"

This was frightening. I'd been here fifteen days, separated from my crew. Had the Germans completely forgotten me?

So each day I scratched my name on my bowl, hoping that one of my crew members would get the same bowl and notice my message. While I watched the jail's front entrance through my small, barred window for hours each day as something to do during the daylight hours, I began to recognize captured airmen leaving whom I had seen arriving a few days before. Some were staying less than a week, and I'd been here for over two weeks. Then I thought of the peephole in my door. I observed that its inside frame was attached with two small screws. I carefully took my spoon and slowly turned the screws with the spoon handle. I removed the small frame and stuck my index finger in far enough to touch the glass. I moved the glass aside so I could see into the hallway. It was scary, so I quickly screwed the framework back into place. Then I remembered that the Hungarian guard would peep through the hole about every four hours. So I decided to remove the frame, shout the names of a few of my crew members, replace the frame, and jump into bed and pretend to be asleep. When I heard the slight noise of the hole's opening the next time, I waited a half hour or so, removed the framework, and yelled through it.

"Lou! Herky! Ellis! Bob!"

Quickly I replaced the framework and jumped into bed. Each day I repeated this procedure; about ten minutes after each yelling session, I could hear the slight noise of the guard as he looked into my cell. By then I was quietly sleeping, so he thought. I hoped one of my crewmen would hear my voice and let the German officers know I was incarcerated here. I was almost certain they'd forgotten me.

For several days I could hear construction noises, the sounds of hammering and sawing outside near the jail. The noise was coming from the left side and I couldn't see anything. But later, Lou, the ball turret gunner, told me that he could see the construction from his cell. A scaffold was being built, and the next day he observed a hanging. Lou said he'd turned his head because it was too gruesome to watch. Then he'd automatically turned his head back to watch just as the rope was cut. I was glad I couldn't observe this from my cell window.

On my fourteenth day in the jail a guard entered my room. Through his motioning and yelling I understood that I was to take the blankets and pillow from my cot and carry them with me. As I left the cell carrying my bedding I was lined up with other prisoners who doing the same. We were marched downstairs and outside to a nearby flat, one-story building. Inside we were told to take off our clothes. Then I realized we were going to take showers. A few months before we were shot down we'd heard rumors about the German concentration camps. An article in the Stars and Stripes, our military newspaper, told of a Jewish man who had escaped from a concentration camp and had written to appeal to President Roosevelt for help. He had reported that the Germans were executing Jews. He told of them being gassed in showers and their bodies being cremated. Because of this I was hesitant to turn on my shower. I waited until others had turned theirs on and then I was prodded by a Hungarian guard. I was greatly relieved when I knew that only water was coming through the showers. Later, as we were returned to our cells, I knew we were being deloused because we had been sprayed with something to kill lice. Our bedding had also been sprayed.

Everyday I continued to put my name and the date on each bowl. I kept looking for the names of my crew members on the bowls I received, but I had no luck. Then on the seventeenth day I saw Bob Hedrick's name and date on a bowl. Below his name and date on the bowl was this message: "Help! Help! I'm starving! My forty-fifth day!"

When we were strip-searched earlier, our belts and shoestrings had been taken from us. When I walked I had to hold up my pants —my waistline had shrunken by at least three inches. This Hungarian diet was a very effective one.

On the afternoon of my nineteenth day in jail, I heard a Hungarian guard calling out a name that sounded vaguely like

Frank Farnsley. I pounded on my cell door with all my strength. My door was opened and I was taken downstairs. In a small room

Frank Farnsley, Top Turret Gunner, 1943

a German officer inter- rogated me. First he said, "Have some chocolate; it's quite good."

"I know, it's from our K rations," I replied, as I gladly accepted it and began to eat.

"We know you are the radio operator on your crew although you denied it earlier," the officer calmly told me.

"I told you the truth," I replied as calmly as possible.

"I don't believe you," he said. "But we already know more about your air force base in Lecce, Italy, than you do. Also we know more names of your pilots than you do."

He boasted as he proceeded to tell me the names of our squadron and group leader, pilot "Killer Kane," and other pilots who were still flying combat missions when we were captured.

"We know each day what your target will be, and that's why we're ready to shoot you down," he continued.

Then I recalled how the Italians who'd been hired to sweep the floors and clean our headquarters back at our base had access to our briefings. I remembered seeing an Italian floor-sweeper out- side our briefing room, and our door was open. Obviously the Italians had radioed this information to the Germans. We were paying them low wages, but the Germans must have been paying them much more!

How grateful I was when my interrogation was over! I was taken to a larger room close by. There sat the rest of my crew, all but Paul, our copilot. Later I learned he'd been taken to a hospital because of his injured ankle and a severe head wound he had received when he was beaten by the Hungarian civilians. Then Lou, our ball turret gunner, told me he had seen my name on one of the aluminum bowls, and he had told the German officer who'd interrogated all of us that I was on his crew. That's why the guard had yelled my name and located me. They didn't even know which cell I was in. Had it not been for Lou, I probably would have broken poor Hedrick's record and been locked up in this jail for more than his forty-five days. How grateful I was!

About a half hour later we were marched about six blocks to the railroad station in Budapest. The Germans had given each of us a loaf of bread and a can of beef. These were our rations for our train ride to prison camp, which turned out to be a six-day and seven-night ride. For some strange reason, the Germans made us carry our parachutes which they'd recovered, as well as a bale of straw for us to sleep on in the boxcar. As we were walking to the railroad station, Hungarian civilians began throwing rocks and brickbats at us as they screamed and yelled. They apparently knew we were captured American airmen, and they were extremely angry with us. We all moved as fast as we could. Most were hit and wounded by the flying missiles of rocks and bricks. In my haste I dropped my bale of straw and was the second of twenty of us to jump into the boxcar. I was about the only one who'd not been injured. Lou shared his bale of straw with me. Soon our train emitted its shrill whistle and we slowly chugged through Budapest. We seemed to be going due west toward Vienna, Austria. Our boxcar had no furniture except our toilet bucket, a five-gallon can which was in one corner. It was for our convenience as we meekly relieved ourselves on our long, slow journey to prison camp. Soon most of us were asleep or in a tired stupor. Our train stopped almost every hour, sometimes more often. Almost all of us had been injured by the barrage of rocks and bricks back in Budapest; bloody faces and bruises on the exposed parts of our bodies attested to that.

At about eight o'clock the next morning our train pulled into the outskirts of Vienna, Austria. After our train came to a stop our boxcar door was opened. The twenty of us were motioned to get out. Somehow, mostly through gestures since we couldn't understand German, the guards made us understand that we could relieve ourselves in the grassy area close to the railroad tracks. I felt quite immodest but relieved as most of us relieved ourselves while Austrian civilians rode by on their bicycles. It was much better than using the smelly can on the boxcar.

After a few minutes we were back in the boxcar and our train pulled into the center of Vienna. We stopped at the choke point, as we called it on our bombing raids. When we'd been at this point fifteen minutes or so, Lou said, "Frank, I hope we get the hell out of here soon because we usually bomb Vienna between 10 and 10:30 A.M.!" And the railroads in Vienna were always one of our targets.

Lou was prophetic; at about ten-fifteen the air-raid sirens sounded loudly. Through the cracks in our boxcar we could see our guards and the civilians running for cover, probably to bomb shelters. Soon there were deafening explosions of bombs, and our boxcar was literally jumping on the tracks. We even heard sounds like gravel or rocks falling on the boxcar. As we knew from previous missions we'd flown over Vienna, the choke point of the railroad yard was the pinpoint of one of three targets we bombed. Fortunately for us, a few small holes in the top of our boxcar was all the damage rendered by this bombing. It was terrible; I doubt that any of us had been more terrified in our lives. I had been silently praying as I, like the others, curled up into a ball with my hands over my head. And I suspect all twenty of us, like a church choir, had been silently praying, almost in unison.

On our boxcar journey of six days and seven nights our food supply was running low, to say the least. We'd devoured our can of beef and also our loaf of hard bread after the first couple of days. On the fifth day as we stopped for about the twentieth time, the German guards gave us each a cup of vegetable soup which contained red, stringy bits of meat. It was delicious! It was the best soup I'd ever eaten, even better than Mom's. Later we learned why. The best food one can eat is when hunger pangs are so great—this slow, gnawing pain that only quits tormenting a person when he is once again eating. Later a mere chunk of bread became the best food I'd ever eaten! And even later, a raw potato or turnip became the most tasty. The taste of food and its satisfaction is definitely determined by the degree of one's hunger as we POWs all learned during our captivity.

Two-thirds of the time our boxcar was waiting in many different German railroad stations; it was obvious that our bombing had been quite successful. Many times we waited while the tracks were repaired. Other times we were side-tracked and waited for hours to be hooked onto another train. German rail transportation was in very poor condition.

On the early afternoon of our seventh day in the boxcar our train pulled into the small town of Kiefheide, located between Danzig, Poland, and Stettin, Germany, about seventy-five miles northeast of Stettin. A German officer was there to greet us, and he told us that we were to get off the boxcar. Then he informed us that we were only about four kilometers from our prison camp and that we'd walk there. The twenty of us were lined up in a column of twos and began our walk. After we'd walked a short distance we noticed trampled food on the ground. We recognized Kraft cheese cartons, Sunkist raisin boxes with mashed raisins inside, other labels, and more trampled American food. We became quite excited because we knew other POWs had walked to this camp. They obviously had so much food that it was scattered all along the way! The thought of an abundance of food made us eager to get to camp because we were beyond being hungry; we felt like we were starving.

About an hour later we came to a large clearing which was surrounded by pine trees and we could see the large buildings of the camp a few hundred yards away. As we approached the camp we saw several hundred American prisoners sitting on the ground outside. When we got closer we were shocked to see that most of them were bleeding and bruised as if they'd been beaten. We were allowed to sit on the ground. In very subdued voices some of them told us what had happened. The German officer in charge of them had made the guards chain their legs together in twos and had turned guard dogs loose on them as they were made to run from the railroad station to the camp. Also the guards stuck many with bayonets. Several had been killed and most were wounded. We were very surprised when the Germans marched the twenty of us into the camp. The hundreds of wounded and bleeding men were still sitting and lying on the ground outside. We were taken to a building on the grounds outside the camp. We were asked our names. Then they had us hold up strips of white cardboard to our chests. My cardboard had the number 5004 written on it. We were photographed and then taken into camp.

Inside the camp we were informed that the barracks were full and that we'd have to put up a tent. German guards gave us instructions as we erected it. It was about twenty feet by twelve feet, just large enough to place twenty straw-filled mattresses, ten on each side, on the ground. It was 20 July 1944. Twenty-six days after being captured we were finally in a POW camp. Two days later we were given two postal cards and were informed that we could write home twice each month. The cards would be censored; nothing about the war or our plight could be written. If we didn't comply our cards would be destroyed. We were given our address: M Stamlager, Kriegsgefangenen Lager, Der Luftwaffe Nr. IV, Deutschland.

The wounded men who were outside the camp were taken to another compound of the camp the next day, and we didn't see any of them again until many months later when we evacuated the camp.

The twentieth of July 1944 was a beautiful day; it was quite warm, probably about eighty-five degrees, and there was a good breeze. We had been given a thick chunk of brown bread, our daily ration, and in the evening we were given a bowl of vegetable soup which had potatoes in it. We were much more content because this was much more food than we'd been given on the boxcar ride. We were also pleased with our sleeping quarters. Each of us was given a straw mattress which we lined up, ten on each side of our tent. We were crowded but did have room enough to stretch out.

In a few days we slowly adjusted to POW life. We learned from the others that we didn't have to work. The Germans were very rank-conscious; they didn't believe in making non-commissioned officers or regular officers do manual labor. So each day we laid around on the grass in the warm sunshine and talked, mostly about our plight, home, and food as we were always hungry. Our meager diet was a good one for losing weight. Having tired of walking around holding up my pants, I managed to use a case knife to cut off the end of one of our tent ropes. From this I made a belt to hold up my pants. I also used small strands of it to make shoelaces.

About a week after arriving at camp my tent mates and I had a problem. Jack, the first in our two rows of straw mattresses on the left side of our tent, came down with crabs. He tried to pick and wash them off; we were allowed to bathe from a bucket. But the next day the one who slept next to him became infected also. So the crabs traveled down the row. Each day the next in line became infected. Then the crabs traveled across to the next ten of us until we were all cursed with crabs! The Germans had given each of us a razor which the American Red Cross had sent. The shaving, along with an application or two of salve of some sort that the Germans gave us, worked wonders. Soon we were "Crab free!"

Almost every day more prisoners arrived. We eagerly watched as they entered the camp to see if we knew anyone. Occasionally one or more from our bomb squadron would arrive and could give us the news from our base. They could tell us who'd been shot down, killed, or was still flying when they abruptly departed their company. Meanwhile I was very happy to meet a childhood friend, James Hemphill, who had been shot down several months before I had. I'd first met James, from Jackson, Mississippi, when both of us were eight years old. James spent weekends with his two first cousins who lived on farms only a half mile from our farm. We had become close friends on his visits. It was great to have someone from back home; we spent time talking about our childhood adventures in his cousin's barn and in the woods nearby. It made our lives a bit more interesting.

One day as we were watching more prisoners being brought into camp, I recognized a high school friend from Florence, Mississippi.

"Marvin Alford!" I exclaimed.

"Frank Farnsley!" he replied, quite surprised. "What are you doing here?"

"I didn't come here on vacation!"

A short time later I gave Marvin what remained of my daily bread ration because he hadn't eaten for several days and the Germans had not given him his bread ration for the day. Marvin and I hugged each other several times, laughed and cried at the same time, and told each other what latest news we knew from back home in Florence. The news wasn't current because I hadn't heard from anyone back home for four months, and it had been about six months since Marvin had gotten any news from his home because he had been shot down a few months before I had.

During the days and weeks that followed, Marvin and I talked every day; we walked around the perimeter of the compound and, bit by bit, told each other about our flying experiences and what happened on our final missions. Marvin had experienced far worse treatment than I. He and the survivors of his crew were shot down over France. Fortunately, at first they were taken by the French Underground and received good treatment. Because the French Underground had rescued so many American flyers, it was months before Marvin and the other survivors of his crew could be marched across the Pyrenees Mountains into Spain and safety. Meanwhile Marvin and his crew members were dressed in French civilian clothes and passed as Frenchmen. They were given concise instructions by the French. Marvin was dressed as a French undertaker. He and his crew members, who were also dressed to represent French occupations, lived with small groups of the French Underground. When they ate in restaurants and met at sidewalk cafes, they were told to never say a word because their American accents would be recognized by the French and, even worse, by the German occupation troops. For almost two months Marvin's crew lived this way. Then, led by two French Underground members, they started their long walk through the Pyrenees Mountains into Spain. Being fed and clothed well they made it through the mountains; it took them about two weeks. Marvin said as they approached the Spanish border that their French guides gave them instructions to wait about a half mile from the end of the road under a large tree in a small clearing because they had to depart at this point. Marvin's group followed these instructions. Reaching the end of the road they relaxed under the specified tree. About five minutes later two German soldiers abruptly appeared with drawn rifles. Marvin and the others were quickly captured by the German soldiers. They had been betrayed. These French guards were double agents. They were collecting money from the American government and were also being paid by the Germans for their betrayals. This must not have been very widely publicized because this was the only time I'd ever heard that some of the French Underground members were traitors. This was another strange aspect of World War II. Marvin and the others were turned over to the German Gestapo who tortured them unmercifully while trying to get the names of the Frenchmen who had taken care of and hidden them in Paris.

Because Marvin and the other captured airmen were never given the real names of these French helpers, they were forced only to reveal the code names of the French. Nevertheless, they were tortured for over a month by the Gestapo. Marvin said their worst torture was the drowning technique. He said that the Gestapo would put their heads into a tub of water, hold them beneath the water until they almost drowned, let them up until they recovered, and continue this procedure for a half hour or more until they would fall to the ground in complete exhaustion or would become unconscious. Other torture techniques were used, but Marvin said this was the worst.

About a month later the Gestapo, having gotten all the information from Marvin and the others, turned them over to the regular German army. Marvin and the other captured American airmen were put into a boxcar. About a week later they joined us at Stalag Luft IV. They were in even worse shape than my crew had been in when we had arrived about two months earlier.

Life as a POW was much the same day after day. We were always hungry and most of our conversation pertained to food. About the first of August 1944 we received our first Red Cross parcels. It was the most exciting and delightful day of our lives as POWs! The Germans told us they'd only received enough parcels for us to have one-half of a parcel each. The parcels contained eleven pounds of food and two packs each of cigarettes. Basically the food contents were a box of raisins or prunes, a can of powdered milk, instant coffee, a can of Spam, a package of crackers, a small can of jam, a chocolate bar, and a half pound of Kraft or Velveeta cheese. Lou and I were partners; we carefully divided a parcel. Lou let me divide it. Then he had first choice of the half he preferred. Dividing the food into halves became an art. Each bit of food was so precious to us. At this point all of us would have fought a duel with anyone who made a disparaging remark about the American Red Cross! For the first three months we each received a half of a parcel each. After that the parcels only came about every two months; then for the last two months none came at all.

Toward the end of the summer we received softballs, bats, footballs, razors and blades, toothbrushes, soap, and even a few musical instruments from the Red Cross and the American YMCA. Also we got some paperback books. My favorite among them were the historical novels. I remember reading Van Wyck Mason's Stars on the Sea and his Rivers of Glory. Also I remember reading Jamaica Inn, but my favorite was Charles Dickens' A Tale of Two Cities, which I had read while in high school, but enjoyed even more the second time. The YMCA also sent us several record players and some records. The musical Oklahoma was among the records. When our turn came to play it our room was allowed to keep Oklahoma for two days. So for two days we listened to it being played over and over, day and night. To this day I know every word of all the songs in this musical, and I've had several dreams about it. Once I even dreamed that I was singing "Oh, What a Beautiful Morning" to a large audience and became famous!

At first almost everyone played softball and touch-football, but many of us soon learned that those of us who played regularly were losing weight fast. Our near-starvation diet along with the strenuous exercise was taking its toll. Soon many of us quit playing. The warm summer days of July, August, and September, we were to learn, were the best months of our incarceration. We'd lie around on the grassy compound and talk about our families and friends back home. Invariably the conversation would get back to foods, favorite ones as well as some basic ones. I remember Rudy (Ozzie) Oswaldt, a good friend from Wisconsin, saying, "I'd give my right arm for a skillet of fried potatoes with onions."

The borderline starvation diet the Germans had us on was just enough to keep us alive. The Germans said that since we didn't have to work we didn't need much food. Learning to cope with the never-stopping, gnawing hunger pangs was no easy task because they never ceased except when we got our meager amount of Red Cross parcels or when we ate our evening cup of soup.

After a few months we no longer got the vegetable soup with potatoes. The Germans said we'd no longer have potatoes because they had to save them for seed potatoes to be planted in early spring. So our soup now was made of dehydrated vegetables which consisted of spinach, cabbage, carrots, and turnips. This mixture had a black juice and could only be eaten when we were extremely hungry. We were, so we ate it; even so, we almost had to force it down.

Each evening at about 6 P.M. one of us would go get our bucket of soup. It was exactly enough for each of us to have one cup. On about the first of October 1944 we were moved from our tents into the barracks. Where there had been twelve men in each room there were now twenty-four. Eight triple-decked bunks crowded the room. We had to turn sideways to get between them. We took turns getting our soup. When I finally got my turn it was quite exciting because the one who got the soup also got to serve it. As the server one would give himself a thick, full cup and also would do the same for his best buddies. We were having our first big snowstorm as I went to get our bucket of soup one evening. The snow was wet and very slippery. Only a few yards from our barrack I slipped on the snow and ice. Although I fell I managed to hold onto the bucket. However, about a third of the vegetable soup with potatoes splashed onto the ground. I was scared. I had to have a full bucket. So I scooped the soup and snow from the ground until the bucket was once again full. I stirred it with my hand. After I'd dished out two or three cups, Liberio, the obnoxious one from the Bronx, yelled, "You son of a bitch! You've spilled our soup! Its full of dirt and straws!"

Fortunately, Lou, Herky, and some other friends protected me from several others who wanted to beat me up. Each ate his soup carefully as he removed bits of straw, dirt, and other debris.

One day, shortly after we'd each gotten our half of a Red Cross parcel, Doyle, "the Needle" as we called him, had made a concoction of powdered milk, prunes, and sugar. Doyle sat his precious bowl of dessert on top of a cardboard box that he'd fastened to the side of his bunk. I was sitting on Lou's bunk which was next to Doyle's. Lou came up from behind and poked me in the ribs. As I was very ticklish I jumped up, hit Doyle's box, and his prune mixture flew in all directions. I felt terrible as Doyle, who was called "the Needle" because he was so skinny and was good-natured enough to provide us with a bit of humor by closing one eye when we called him that, sat down on his bunk and cried. Most of the others laughed. I gave Doyle what prunes and powdered milk and sugar I had left, but unfortunately there wasn't much since I hadn't been as conservative as he had.

Each morning and afternoon the Germans would take a head count of us. Because the "Great Escape" had taken place a few months earlier about a hundred miles from us where the officers from our crew were POWs, the Germans were making sure no escapes took place in our camp. So we were lined up and counted twice each day. Invariably we'd be one or two short each time we were counted. The German guards would search the barracks and roust out a few who were sleeping in their bunks. As punishment these sleepyheads would be tried in court which was held about every two weeks. When court was held we were all lined up in our usual formation of five men deep, and the German judge would loudly announce the name and sentence each rule violator received.

"Sergeant James Crenshaw, you get forty days mit hard conditions for cutting a tent rope! You destroyed property of the Third Reich!"

Forty days mit hard conditions meant each guilty one would be put into a six-foot by eight-foot room and would get only bread and water for forty days. If one were thin before, and all of us were, he'd be almost a walking skeleton as he was returned to quarters after "Forty days mit hard conditions!"

In about mid-August of 1944 the Germans excavated a large area of about one hundred feet by fifty feet in the center of our compound. When the rectangular area had been completely finished, we observed that it was about four feet deep. We asked the guards what it was for, but they just remained silent. Rumors started among us that it was to be a swimming pool for us. Some actually believed it. When a concrete lining was poured, the Germans told us it was our water supply in case of a fire. When the "pool" was finally filled with water, a couple of daredevil POWs jumped in and swam a bit. They were quickly rousted out of it by German guards with fixed bayonets. However, the Germans allowed us to play around the edges of the pool, and some of us made small sailboats out of various scraps of wood and paper. On windy days sailboat races were held. Cigarettes had become our "money," so much betting was taking place on the races. If one didn't have cigarettes he could use Red Cross food for his betting.

There was another exciting event which was quite amusing in its beginning stages. One day, early in our captivity, we were startled by a huge explosion. It sounded like a cannon being fired. Many of us cautiously approached the area in our compound from which the noise had come. Just beside our outdoor latrine a team of horses was parked, hooked to a wagon. A large hose about eight inches in diameter had been inserted into the latrine. Then one of the German guards lit a mechanism with a long match. Suddenly there was a loud explosion followed by a noisy, sucking, gurgling sound. Obviously the contents of the latrine were being drawn up into the large tank. This was their ingenious method of cleaning the latrines. Soon the wagon drawn by the team of horses slowly lumbered out through our camp gate. The Germans informed us that the contents from the latrine were used to fertilize their potatoes and other crops. This soon became known as the "Honey Wagon" routine.

Because of previous escape attempts from POW camps, the German soldiers went all over our compound punching a slender rod about six feet long into the ground. They were looking for possible tunnels. A poster was placed in each barrack which said,

"Escapes from POW camps have ceased to be a foolish game. All POWs attempting to escape will be shot!"

As we became hungrier each day, every bit of edible food was consumed. We'd learned to glean the carrot and turnip tops and collect the potato peelings from the waste containers outside the kitchen where our food was prepared. When we had first received Red Cross parcels, the POWs were disposing of their prune seeds. I began picking them up from the compound ground. I'd crack the prune seeds and eat them. Hardly a day passed before someone observed me cracking the seeds. Within a few days no one was throwing away prune seeds; they were being eaten by their owners. Because I didn't smoke I traded my cigarettes from the Red Cross parcels for food. Two cigarettes were worth about two medium-sized slices of bread, or a chunk of cheese about the size of a cubic inch, or a comparable piece of Spam, or a nut cup full of raisins or prunes. Many who were seriously addicted to nicotine would trade as much as a fourth of their Red Cross food for cigarettes.

At about 3 A.M. in mid-December of 1944 we were abruptly awakened by German guards; they were searching our barrack. As usual we weren't told what they were trying to find, but we assumed they were looking for our crystal radio set, which had been made by several POWs. This radio set provided us with BBC war news and was greatly appreciated by all of us. The radio set had been assembled so that it could be quickly taken apart, and each of four or five pieces was given to different POWs. This way it would be difficult for the Germans to find and confiscate all the parts. Replacement parts were available in case they did. The Germans had been quite inconsistent when we'd been searched. All belts, shoelaces, and electric flying suits had been taken from our crew members. Other POWs had hardly been searched at all. Some were allowed to keep their electrically heated suits, which contained copper wires. A few even kept their helmets, which had radio headsets. Each night, about a half hour after our barracks were bolted shut and the lights were turned off, our barrack leader would, in an audible whisper, read us the latest BBC news. What a great morale booster! Based on the latest news we thought the Germans would surely surrender by Christmas of 1944. During this search and others that followed the Germans never found our radio set. One day the Germans made a surprise daylight inspection. Those in charge of the radio set didn't have time to take it apart. The POW with the radio set had it in a cardboard box and was walking slowly across our compound. A guard stopped him and said, "Was ist das?"

The POW calmly replied, "It's our radio set."

The guard chuckled and said, "Ja, ja, I thought it was," as he walked away.

Soon after cigarettes became our chief medium of exchange, the trading and then gambling became common. Many POWs were betting on sailboat races. A POW from New York established a numbers racket. Bets were being placed on all sorts of trivia, such as which barrack would win the softball and touch-football tournaments. The New Yorker and his two assistants soon became quite wealthy, in our way of thinking. They had enough cigarettes to buy ample Red Cross food and were the only ones who were no longer losing weight.

Other than those who became seriously ill with such maladies as pneumonia, typhus fever, and amoebic dysentery who were taken to the camp hospital and were seldom seen again, there were a few tragedies that were different. Around each of our four camp compounds, each one of which contained approximately two thousand five hundred men, there was a warning wire about ten feet inside our barbed wire enclosure. We were told never to cross this wire which was actually a narrow strip of timber that had been staked about two feet off the ground. On one occasion when most of us were outside, a distraught POW who had apparently "cracked up" jumped across the warning strip and began tugging on the barbed wire fence. Immediately a guard in the nearby tower opened fire with his machine gun. Our fellow POW's body was riddled with bullets as he clung to the fence for a few seconds and then slowly fell to the ground. An occasional event of this nature caused much brooding and depression among us.

Because we were securely locked inside our barrack after dark, we usually were awake from two to four hours before all of us POWs settled down and went to sleep. During these hours many talked about their lives back home. Some tried to outdo others with their unusual flight combat stories. And, of course, some few bragged about their sexual encounters, mostly on the rare occasions when we had enough to eat to satisfy our hunger.

The most unusual true story was told by a POW from another barrack. A friend of mine who was in the same room with him told me the following true story.

As the B-24s were dropping their bombs on a target in Budapest, Hungary, the bombardier asked Joe, a waist gunner on his crew, to stick his head out the waist window to see if his bombs hit the target. As Joe stuck his head out the window his steel helmet got caught on the edge of the window. Joe ducked his head to loosen the helmet. As he did his flack suit which wasn't fastened flipped out the window just as he ducked his head out the window. The flack suit got caught in the "slip stream" which is the gush of air created by the engines. Joe was instantly pulled from the plane. Fortunately, Joe had his parachute on and immediately pulled its rip cord. Joe's tail gunner waved goodbye to him as he drifted down in his parachute. Joe had to be begged and cajoled to get him to relate his story. We all thought it was so dumb of his bombardier to think Joe could see and follow his bombs all the way to the target with so many bombs being dropped simultaneously by all the planes. Joe was the only POW in our camp of ten thousand men who didn't get shot down—he fell out of his plane!

As Christmas of 1944 approached there was excitement in our camp. Rumors circulated that we would get a full, special food parcel from the Red Cross. A few days before Christmas we did get a half parcel each. This plus the fact that we heard over BBC radio news that the war would be over soon created much hope and excitement.

TSgt. Mears, an ordained minister from Texas who had church services and Bible study for us each week, helped us plan a Christmas program which the Germans approved. It was to be the traditional Christmas story—the birth of Jesus in Bethlehem. Word was spread among us that at the end of our program we would sing a special song. The Germans approved our program but didn't know about our plan for all to sing at the conclusion. The program was a big success. At the conclusion, a few bars of our song were played; we all joined in and sang "God Bless America." This beautiful song made most of us cry; it was so meaningful to us at that moment. It echoed through the cold, damp air and could be heard from miles away. So began our Christmas of 1944. No doubt it was probably the saddest Christmas most of us would ever experience.

At this point I'll digress and relate the fate of the three surviving officers on our crew. I met Paul Stillions at our Ninety-eighth Bomb Group's reunion in Colorado Springs, Colorado, in 1987. He related to me the following account of their experiences while they were POWs in Luft III, an officers' camp:

David Himes, Paul Stillions, and Robert Moore were taken to Luft III which was located about a hundred miles from our camp. It was from Luft III that the "Great Escape" took

Paul Stillions, Copilot, 1943

place. Many of you have probably seen the movie based on this true story. According to the latest verification Paul was able to get about a year ago, one man is still living who reached freedom through this escape. Of the approximately fifty men who escaped only three survived, and two of them have died since the war. The rest were shot by the Germans while escaping. This event occurred about two months before our crew officers were incarcerated there.

Paul bailed out of our plane at an altitude of about four thousand feet. By the time he and David were ready to jump, our plane was descending rapidly at a sharp angle. Paul tried to open the bomb bay doors, their only possible escape exit. The doors were jammed, so Paul jumped on them with both feet. The doors ripped partly open, and his body was left hanging because the doors hadn't opened completely. After a brief struggle the doors opened enough so that

1st Lt. David Himes with his wife, Merle, 1945

he fell through. Then Lieutenant Himes jumped. As Paul approached the ground he observed that some of us who'd already landed were being chased and beaten by the Hungarian civilians. He landed feet first which resulted in a badly sprained right ankle. Before he could be rescued by German soldiers Paul was beaten by the civilians; fortunately his bloody head wound was not too serious. His ankle sprain, however, was extremely painful. Soon Paul was brought to the small village where Bob Moore and I were in the small courtyard being guarded by German soldiers. A few minutes later, Lieutenant Himes was brought there. He'd also been beaten by the civilians. On 28 June 1944 Paul was taken from the jail in Budapest. He was put into a military hospital nearby. Then on 6 July 1944 the military hospital was hit by bombs dropped by our planes, B-24s from the Fifteenth Air Force stationed in various parts of southern Italy, including our Ninety-eighth Bomb Group from Lecce, Italy. Paul was transferred to another hospital in Budapest and remained there until 11 July 1944. Then he was taken back to the Budapest jail where the survivors of our crew were. He, Lieutenant Himes, and Lieutenant Moore were taken by boxcar with other American officers to Luft III in Sagan, Germany. They arrived at Luft III on 26 July 1944.

Paul revealed that life in Luft III where the ten thousand American POW officers were quartered was much like our lives in Luft IV. The big difference was that the Germans gave them more Red Cross parcels than we received. Even so, they too were constantly hungry. Paul said that because the "Great Escape" had happened only two months before their arrival, shortly after they got to Luft III they were taken and shown the tunnel from which the fifty officers had attempted to escape. After a wild chase over the German countryside, the escaping men were killed by the Germans. Of the three men who escaped it's reported that only one is still living.

In Luft III our officers also had gotten a larger supply of books, record players and records, softballs, bats, toothbrushes, etc., from the American Red Cross and the YMCA than we enlisted men received because the Germans were very rank-conscious even with us POWs. Like we enlisted men, our officers were lined up in columns of five and counted twice a day. Everyone had to be present or accounted for; the only ones who weren't present were those who had become very ill and were in the hospital.

In mid-January of 1945 the Russians began their long-awaited winter offense as the temperature hit a new below-zero level. The Russians took Warsaw and Krakow in Poland and advanced on Posen and Breslau. In Luft III many prisoners thought that they'd be liberated by the oncoming Russians, and many felt that they'd be evacuated from the camp. Those who felt that they'd be marched from the camp made preparations. Some made over-shoes out of an extra pair of socks with tin-can soles which could be tied over their shoes, several made mittens by stuffing German toilet paper between layers of cloth, and others insulated their two blankets with toilet paper. Backpacks were made by sewing a stocking on the top of a bag and on the bottom and attaching a cloth belt as a strap. Paul said that fortunately they were unaware of Hitler's order that all POWs' shoes would be taken from them before they started their march. It was also very fortunate for the POWs that the Germans realized at this time that they'd lost the war and so disobeyed Hitler's order. The prisoners were allowed to keep their shoes. Very few, if any, would have survived the walk during sub-zero weather otherwise.

By 27 January 1945 the Russians were closing in on Breslau and Steinau. At about 9 P.M. the Germans announced to those in Luft III the following order: "At eleven o'clock tonight you will begin a march to a new location. Use the two hours to prepare yourselves."

The prisoners in Luft III, including Lieutenant Himes, our pilot, Lieutenant Stillions, our copilot, and Lieutenant Moore, our navigator, rushed around making packs, packing what little food and clothing they possessed, throwing away useless articles. Some even made sleds by using bed slats for the runners and platform. On this they could drag their prized possessions.

At about 3 A.M. on 30 January 1945 the Germans rousted the prisoners out of their barracks for instructions. They were told that they'd walk in a column of five and that there would be no stragglers. There were numerous guards and trained dogs to enforce the rules. Also they were informed that no one should attempt to escape; anyone who tried would be shot.

Slowly the ten thousand prisoners departed from Luft III. The sad memories of their lives there were not left behind. For the rest of their lives these memories would be etched in their brains!

As the Luft III prisoners walked along Highway 94, they met the once-mighty Wehrmacht Ski Troopers, all dressed in white.

These "supermen" were begging cigarettes from the POWs. They seemed to range in age from teenagers to about fifty years old and were headed for the Russian front. The prisoners reached Halbau at about two in the afternoon where they saw many French forced-laborers. The temperature was below zero, and some of the men had frostbitten feet and hands. Finally, about two thousand of the prisoners, including Paul, were crowded into a church. It was so crowded that they had to sleep in shifts.

The Germans gave them cold meat and crackers which were quickly devoured. Cold, stiff, and hungry, they left Halbau at dawn and trudged wearily past Freiweldou. There was a long, sloping hill running through town, and most had trouble making it. Then they came to flat farmland which was easier to traverse, but the bitterly cold wind blew right through them. Finally the prisoners came to a small village where they were housed in large barns, about fifty men to a barn. The barns were so crowded that they could not sleep all at the same time, so some would stand and walk around slowly while others slept. Even inside the barns it was very cold, and they ate Red Cross food they'd carried with them. Many, by this time, had diarrhea; "accidents" gave a nauseating stench to the air in the barns. The prisoners stayed in the village an extra day. The Germans allowed them to dry our their socks, shoes, and clothes. They put the wet clothes next to their bodies as they slept to help dry them. The prisoners mended their shoes, packs, and mittens as best as they could. Also some did a little trading with the German civilians for onions, hot water, potatoes, and ersatz coffee in exchange for cigarettes and soap.

On 31 January 1945 the Luft III prisoners walked twenty-nine kilometers through rain and snow. The weather changed rapidly from rain to snow, back and forth, which made walking miserable in the now hilly countryside. From late January of 1945 until the prisoners arrived at Stalag 7A, life was quite redundant. They slept in barns and walked from ten to twenty miles a day. Sometimes they slept in churches or abandoned buildings. Diarrhea was rampant. The German civilians were upset because many of the prisoners had to stop along the streets of towns and villages to have uncontrollable bowel movements. Paul said that on 7 February 1945 they were put into the north lager of the camp. This lager soon became known as "The Snake Pit." Six hundred men were put into a run-down building with no beds and no heat. By this time most were sick. Their bodies were covered with fleas and lice. There was not sufficient room for everyone to lie down simultaneously, and what food they were given was cold. From 8 February through 10 February of 1945 these six hundred prisoners stayed in "The Snake Pit." A few made hammocks out of their blankets and got some sleep. Then on 11 February 1945 all were strip-searched. The Germans were quite excited; they got hammers, maps, nails, wrenches, and other items that had been picked up by the prisoners along the way. Most of these items were taken from a brick factory where the prisoners had stayed. Then the prisoners were deloused, given a shower, and put into an east lager barrack. There were tiers of twelve men, three bunks high. The bunks had straw mattresses and were full of lice, fleas, and bedbugs. Their de-lousing had been useless! So began their miserable lives in Mooseburg, Germany, in Stalag 7A. The weather continued to be very cold and damp. Most of the men stayed in bed all day to keep warm because the Germans gave them no fuel for heat. There were no facilities with which to do anything if anyone did get out of bed. Because they were so crowded most of them put their few personal belongings into a handmade bag and hung it from the ceiling. The German food rations consisted of a cup of warm water for breakfast, a cup of thin soup for dinner, and a chunk of black bread for dinner. At first they got no Red Cross parcels, and everyone was very skinny. These POW officers were then quite lucky. They began receiving a Red Cross parcel, eleven pounds of delicious food every two weeks. Along with their German rations they were now being fed more than they'd gotten before. At first these prisoners were given British Red Cross parcels, which contained food that must be cooked. But the Germans gave them no fuel, so these men, determined to cook their food, made burners and blowers from the tin cans saved from the Red Cross parcels. For fuel they burned some of their bed slats. When they'd used all the slats they could (enough had to be left to keep the beds from collapsing), sabotage work was done: the men began tearing out and using wood from the inner floor. Also sticks of wood were stolen from their toilet which was a slit trench over which they squatted while relieving themselves. The Germans refused to clean out these trench latrines until they overflowed onto the parade grounds. Flea, lice, and bedbug bites covered the men's bodies and caused serious bacterial infections as the men scratched. Some became very ill with these infections. Most had worn the same clothes for four to six weeks. They were filthy and, of course, insect-infected.

As spring finally arrived the renewed offensive of the Allies began pushing the Germans deeper into the center of Germany. In late April the prisoners observed American fighter planes scouting their camp, and on 29 April 1945 Paul said all prisoners were ordered to go inside the barracks. They could hear artillery and even rifle and machine gun fire. Paul also said that through cracks in the walls they observed, much to their delight, Allied infantrymen advancing toward their camp and also pushing toward Mooseburg. Soon the prisoners heard the most exciting sound they'd heard in years, the rumble of American tanks! When these tanks rolled into the prison compound, Paul stated, thunderous shouts, cheers, whistles, and applause arose which probably could be heard several miles away. Suddenly a hush fell over the compound; all eyes turned toward nearby Mooseburg. Then almost twenty thousand eyes saw machine gun bullets splatter against the church steeple nearby. After a brief moment of silence, the scene caused tears to stream from the eyes of every POW. Those men saw the greatest sight, felt the most emotional moment of their lives! Before their eyes, and flying beautifully above one of the church steeples, was the symbol of their beloved country, the American flag!

"No doubt," Paul said. "Never again will I ever see ten thousand men cry!"

About the only difference in our lives back at Luft IV from those of our officers at Luft III was that we didn't get half as many Red Cross parcels as they did. However, the Germans fumigated our barracks at Luft III, and we didn't have lice and bedbugs. Overall the Germans, because of their rank-consciousness, fed the officers more than the semi-starvation diet we received.

With twenty-four of us crowded into a room about fourteen by sixteen feet, our lives became more and more chaotic as winter arrived. Because of the cold most of us stayed inside during the day; several crew members and I took a couple of brief, daily walks around the compound to get a bit of exercise and to get away from the foul atmosphere of our room. We had become so accustomed to the stench of body odor that we could only smell it each time we returned from our walks.

By late January of 1945 we began to hear the faint rumble of heavy gunfire coming from the east. It sounded like far away thunder. We knew this was coming from the eastern front. Our BBC radio broadcasts reported that the Russians were advancing deep into Poland and that the battles were fierce. Great excitement permeated our camp. Some began making bets as to when the Russians would arrive and liberate us. Most of us felt it would happen within a week or ten days. Our spirits were at the highest peak they'd reached since our imprisonment.

On 31 January 1945 after we had been counted in the afternoon, a German officer announced to us that we would evacuate our camp in a few days. He gave us orders to be prepared to leave on short notice.

The thunderous sounds of gunfire from the eastern front became louder and closer each day. Our camp literally became a beehive of activity. Everyone was busy preparing for our evacuation. We practiced getting our meager belongings together so we could carry them. We learned from each other. Our two blankets were rolled tightly crosswise so that they could be slung around the neck and under one arm. The sleeves of our spare shirts were sewn together, and the bottom of the shirt tail was sewn shut to form a bag to hold what little precious food and other articles we possessed.

Early on the morning of 5 February 1945 the German guards burst into our barrack shouting, "Roust! Roust! Schnell! Schnell!"

We were taken to the end of the compound and marched through the gate. In a large clearing outside the camp about seven thousand of us were lined up in columns of five. This procedure had taken the better part of an hour. Those among us who were quite sick, had lost a limb, or who'd been seriously wounded were not with us. We'd heard that about three thousand sick or wounded would be put on boxcars and would leave by train.

At about 8:30 A.M. on 5 February 1945 a German captain ordered us to be quiet and began to give orders to this massive group of approximately seven thousand of us. He barked out lengthy orders, rules, and regulations that we would follow, in fairly good but broken English. About all we needed to remember was that we were to march in columns of five and that there would be no stragglers. The captain informed us that there were many German guards and well trained guard dogs to enforce the rules. He also informed us that escaping as a POW had ceased to be a foolish American game and that anyone attempting to escape would be shot. Both the guards and the dogs were there in abundance for us to see.

As soon as the German commandant had finished his crisp, lengthy speech of orders and instructions, a few seconds of complete silence was followed with a loud "Baa, baa, baa," an excellent imitation of a sheep's call sounding through the cold, damp air.

The German captain screamed as only an infuriated German officer can, "Find that man and shoot him!"

After a futile search and much confusion, especially loud talking and yelling by shaken German guards, we and the Germans finally became quiet as the German captain said, "Another incident of disrespect for the Third Reich like this and ten of you will be immediately shot!"

Our march began, but before we had gone thirty paces a German officer who was riding a bicycle slipped on the ice and snow and fell quite hard on the frozen, snow-covered ground. A roaring noise, in cheering fashion, along with shrill whistling, arose from the throats of most of us seven thousand POWs. The noise must have rivaled that which came from the spectators at the Roman Coliseum almost two thousand years ago when the Christians were thrown to the lions. After another tongue-lashing by the German commandant, we finally began our long, bleak journey, which did provide many humorous situations but also cost the lives of many of our buddies, as well as causing much suffering for all of us.

Our first day's march of about fifteen miles went quite well; most of us had saved enough Red Cross food to satisfy our hunger. We were allowed to stop and sit down for a ten-minute break at mid-morning and mid-afternoon. As nightfall approached we stopped and were put into barns for the night. About three hundred of us were in each barn. Because the German villages and towns were usually only about ten miles apart and the distances to each were marked in kilometers, we knew about how far we walked each day. After we were in the barns, the Germans would bring us hot water and also would empty a couple of bushels of boiled potatoes on the ground inside the barn. The potatoes would be our evening meal for about a month. Most of us in this early stage of the march had instant coffee which we'd saved from our Red Cross food. A tin can we'd kept which had contained powdered milk served as our only bowl from which to eat our potatoes. We had no salt for the potatoes, but after a few nights in the barns someone discovered muriate of salt, a fertilizer which the Germans used for some of their crops. A little of this salty fertilizer sprinkled on the potatoes made them taste better.

On the second day's march we all noticed that our legs and bodies in general began aching. We were not accustomed to so much exercise. In a few more days this aching left as we adjusted to more exercise.

For most of us the first week's walk was not too bad. We had enough Red Cross food to supplement our boiled potatoes so that our hunger wasn't too bad. But then the Red Cross food ran out. Now our daily diet of boiled potatoes and a cup of hot water was not sufficient to satisfy our hunger. To make matters worse, the Germans always emptied the boiled potatoes on the ground inside the barns. As we became hungrier our manners quickly departed. To get any potatoes at all we had to dive at the mound of potatoes and grab all we could. In the wild scramble many of the potatoes were mashed into the straw and manure which covered the floor of the barn. Hungry young men were losing all their manners. The situation became like Darwin's "survival of the fittest." We were regressing to our animal state. Those of us whose physical condition was fairly good got potatoes; the weaker ones got very few, some none. Fortunately we discovered wheat and rye in most of the barns. Most of us had a second pair of socks; we filled these socks with the wheat and rye. As we walked wearily along on our march we could partially satisfy our hunger pangs by chewing the wheat and rye, like so many cows chewing their cud.

In spite of the hunger and other hardships of our plight, as we trudged across the German countryside day after day most of us maintained a sense of humor. Among the amusing examples of humorous incidents which occurred during our march was "the Case of the Redheaded, Washed-out Luftwaffe Cadet." A friendly, quite handsome six-footer, this German guard asked us to teach him English as we trudged along. Two of my buddies agreed to teach him. Since this German knew only a few words of English, my pals decided to have some fun. Soon the red-headed German was repeating as we plodded along, "I'm a SOB. I'm a SOB."

As he was praised by his instructors he responded and raised his voice as he repeated the sentence over and over. And much to the delight of all of us who were within hearing distance, he was given several other sentences to learn, all too filthy to appear in print, as we ambled along.

About the third week of our journey we slept in barns that obviously were infested with body lice because we all came down with them. For me and the others the first few days and nights were really miserable. We were scratching constantly. The lice were about one-fourth as big as a bed bug, so when we stopped to rest along the way, if it wasn't too cold, we'd remove our shirts and pick and kill the lice. But the more lice we killed the more there seemed to be to take their place. I was so exhausted that it got so I could scratch and sleep at the same time. Because our sleep was constantly disturbed by the lice, we became even more exhausted. At about this time the Germans no longer gave us potatoes because, they told us, they were saving them for seed potatoes to be planted soon. Now our food supply from them was a cup of imitation coffee each morning and sometimes at night. Fortunately most of the German barns in which we slept had a good supply of raw potatoes, wheat, and rye. This became our food supply. Because some of the barns contained no potatoes or grain that we could locate, most of us would fill our bags, which would hold about a peck of potatoes, and an extra sock or two with grain when we slept in the well-supplied barns.

Usually we were warm enough when we slept in the barns. We were so crowded that body heat and straw provided sufficient heat. However, one night late in February not enough barns were available for all, so many of us had to sleep outdoors. The ground was snow-covered and it was very cold; the temperature dropped below zero. Two of us put one blanket on the ground and the others on top. Our body heat wasn't enough. It was too cold to sleep. We were afraid we'd freeze to death, so most of us stayed awake. The next day there was talk that several had died during the night. It was difficult to walk because we were so tired from the lack of sleep.

A few incidents that occurred on our march were both amusing and pathetic. One such incident happened on a very cold night. I entitled it, "A Blanket for a Loaf of Bread." Through the American Red Cross each of us had been given two army blankets while in POW camp. Although the winter in our camp was very cold, we were warm enough at night because there were twenty-four of us in a room about fourteen feet by sixteen feet. We were bedded down in eight triple-deck bunks which had four, and only four, slats each. If one were caught with five or more slats in his bed he was given "forty days mit hard conditions." This meant being locked up in a six foot by eight foot cubbyhole and receiving a chunk of bread and water each day. In each room we also had a small stove and we were given twelve peat bricks a day for fuel. To walk within our room we had to turn sideways to move between the bunks.

One night after we had walked one of our longest most grueling treks through a miserable snowstorm, about three hundred of us were herded, cattle fashion as usual, into a large barn. Each of us was very tired and did our usual scrambling, pushing, and fighting for dry straw to construct our usual beds. We tried to locate sufficient room for stretching out among this mass of humanity. Four of us who were good buddies and had become closer than most brothers while living together in the small room in our prison camp had managed to stay together on the march.

"Give me your other blanket so I can fix our sack," said Lou, the ball turret gunner on our crew.

Rudy (Ozzie) Oswaldt from Milwaukee said, "I lost it."

"You lost it? How could you lose something as big as a damned blanket!" yelled Lou.

Finally Ozzie said, "I traded it to a German guard for a loaf of bread."

"You idiot! Give me my half of the bread!" shouted Lou.

"Really, I'm sorry, Lou. I was so hungry I ate it all," Ozzie said meekly.

"You SOB, you can freeze to death. You're not sharing my blankets!" screamed Lou.

Late into the night Ozzie could be heard moaning and groaning and repeating over and over, "Please Lou, let me sleep with you!" After a short pause, Ozzie continued, "I'm freezing to death!" as he sat like an early American Indian with his one blanket wrapped around him.

Lou's only reply was, "Freeze, you stingy SOB!"

After several hours, Lou felt sorry for Ozzie and said, "Okay, crawl over here, but I should let you freeze. It's an easier way to go than starving to death!"

So ended another miserable night of trying to sleep while scratching a thousand or so body lice that slowly crawled and then paused to continue their relentless feasting on our tired bodies.

After our usual long walk on about our fiftieth day, which was a chilly, rainy one in early April, we stopped at barns. Because the sunshine had suddenly appeared and we were soaking wet, the Germans allowed us to sit outside the barn and dry out. Many of us sat on woodpiles because the ground was wet. Someone in one of the immediate groups with which I was sitting kicked several sticks of wood. As he did so he uncovered tin cans that were unopened. This POW took his broken case knife (many of us had one) and opened the can. To our delight it contained cooked beef! About a dozen or so of us grabbed cans and proceeded to open them. Just after I had begun to stuff myself with this delicious meat, a German guard observed us.

"Was ist das?" he asked.

No one answered.

The guard called other guards, and there was much shouting among them. Then the guard in charge who spoke English gave us orders to return the cans of meat. By this time the German farmer who owned the farm came out and talked to the guards.

He told them how many cans of meat he had covered in the wood-pile. After a quick count the farmer said that eleven cans of meat were missing. Immediately we were ordered to return the missing cans. About half of us reluctantly returned our cans. Most of them had been opened and partially devoured. Then in loud orders we were told by the German in charge that we must return all the cans and that for each can that was not returned, ten of us would be shot. All but one can of meat was returned.

"One can of meat is missing!" shouted the guard. "I will count to ten, and if this can is not returned, ten of you will be shot. Eins, zwei, drei . . . . " The German counted to ten.

The missing can was not returned.

"Count off ten men to be shot!" shouted the German.

There was a wild scramble of POWs running toward the rear of our group. No one wanted to be among the ten. Several of our group yelled for the one who had the missing can of meat to return it. One POW yelled, "You SOB, would you let ten of us be shot for a can of meat?"

"Anyone who moves will be shot!" yelled the German in charge.

Again the guard began counting off ten men. Before he had gotten to ten, a POW quite sheepishly walked forward and hand-ed the German the missing can. A loud chorus of "boos" greeted the hungry man who had so reluctantly given up the precious meat.

A few days later we trudged through the German countryside during another rainy day. Once again, because we were soaking wet and so were the guards, we were allowed to sit outside our barn and dry out a while since sunshine had once again appeared. As we were sitting there I noticed several mounds of dirt about four feet high. I had grown up on a farm, and these mounds of dirt reminded me of the ones my Dad had made in which to bury potatoes to keep during the winter. I cautiously began digging my hands into the dirt, hoping not to be detected by the German guards. Having dug about a foot deep, I felt what I thought were potatoes. On further digging, I exposed a kohlrabi. These resembled turnips and were fairly good to eat raw. I uncovered several of them, and my buddy next to me also uncovered several. Soon many of us were digging like gophers and were filling our bags with them. Although the guards who were only a few paces away saw what we were doing, they didn't say a word, but just watched us. Some even smiled as we wiped the dirt off and began eating this greatly appreciated food. The German farmer was not to be seen, so we took all we wanted. I had enough of them, about fifteen pounds, to last a week or so. After this we always dug into the mounds we found; sometimes they were inside the barns. We also, much to our delight, found carrots, potatoes, and turnips. By this time these raw vegetables were all we had to eat. Because dysentery was so prevalent among our group (at least three-fourths of us had it), this diet of raw vegetables made it even worse. The only medicine the Germans gave those with dysentery was charcoal. Eating it did seem to help some of our men.

One night when we were bedded down in a barn after this outbreak of amoebic dysentery had about reached its peak, one POW went to the barn door and shouted, "Posten, schizen, schizen!"

Before the guard could open the door we heard the sound of someone relieving himself.

"You SOB, you shit all over me!" Although there were some sounds of laughter among us, most of us felt sorry for the sick one.

Many of our group became seriously ill and died of this dysentery. It was a pathetic sight, young men wasting away and slowly dying. Almost every morning we saw that several of our men had died during the night. Their bodies, like so many chunks of wood, were tossed into a wagon which was pulled by horses. The very ill had to ride with these corpses of their buddies until the Germans stopped all of us and counted off a burial detail of POWs who were forced to bury their comrades in fields in the German countryside. This procedure continued for the duration of our eighty-seven day march.

On the lighter side, we had one delightful overnight stay in a large German barn. We were bedded down in a dairy barn which contained about twenty milk cows. After we were locked up for the night I took my tin can and crawled slowly into the section of the barn which contained the cows who were neatly lined up in their individual stalls. Since I had grown up on a farm where we always had four or five milk cows, I was quite good at milking. Slowly, trying not to make much noise, I began to milk a cow, using my tin can as a container. But the noise of the milk striking the bottom of my can aroused several of my buddies.

"He's milking a cow!" someone exclaimed.

Immediately I was joined by ten or more others, a few of whom had grown up on farms and knew how to milk cows. But most didn't know how to milk.

"How do you do this?" someone asked. "I squeeze the tit and nothing comes out!"

Soon there was a chorus of milk striking the bottom of tin cans, much to the joy of the successful milkers. I had never liked warm milk fresh from a cow, but this was the best milk I'd ever tasted. After I had drunk about a quart or so I milked more and gave it to my buddies who couldn't milk.

There were several humorous incidents as some tried unsuccessfully to milk. One buddy from New York yelled, "This SOB kicked me!" I noticed that he was milking on the wrong side of the cow. Another said, "How do you turn this tit on? Nothing comes out for me."

For an hour or so those of us who could milk did so, and everyone shared with the others. Soon all the cows were milked dry, and we settled down for the most peaceful sleep we'd had in several months.

At about five o'clock the next morning, the German dairy farmer and his wife came into the barn to milk their cows. After a moment or two the silence was broken by the farmer.

"Was ist das?" he asked. "Mein Gott im Himmel!" he shouted.

In German, which we could partially understand, he soon exclaimed and yelled that all his cows had been milked by the kriegsgefangenen. He reported this to the German guards outside the barn; the guards thought it was amusing, one of them even laughed. The farmer and his wife, after much ranting and raving and swearing at us, calling us American "Schweinehunde," went into their farmhouse. Shortly after, just at daybreak, we were rousted out to begin another dreary day of walking.

On one occasion in late April 1945 our day's journey turned into a real tragedy. At about mid-afternoon as we stopped for our ten-minute rest along the side of the road, we saw two fighter planes coming toward us. Since we'd all had extensive training in aircraft identification, we knew they were our planes, P-51 fighters. At first we were elated: our fighter pilots would report us to ground troops, and we'd be liberated! But then lightning struck! Both planes made a pass over us and opened fire! They'd mistaken us for German troops! All of us wildly scrambled and rolled over on the grassy land beside the road. The P-51 pilots must have known they'd made a mistake as they flew away, not to return. When our panic subsided I saw two of my friends lying motionless, bleeding profusely, dead or dying! Most of us were sobbing uncontrollably or were in a stupor or in shock. We never knew how many were killed and wounded, because our group was stretched out for a mile or so. A German guard counted off a burial detail to bury our dead companions along the side of the road. Fortunately I was never chosen to be on a burial detail; I don't believe I could have survived one, especially one for my good friends! This day, for me, was among the worst days of my almost eleven months of incarceration.

On the morning of 15 April 1945 shortly after we were aroused and prepared to make another bleak day's journey, we heard several Germans talking louder than usual. Then one of them showed us a German newspaper. The headline, in bold, large print, read: "Roosenfeldt, Der Grosse Jude, ist Tot!"

Word of President Franklin Roosevelt's death greatly saddened us because most of us greatly admired him. While many of us were wondering how he'd died and were spreading the word of his death among others, shouting erupted from the German officer in charge of us.

"Find Herman Strietburger!" he exclaimed. "Where is he? Find him immediately!"

Then we learned that Herky, the radio operator on our crew who spoke fluent German, and two of his friends had escaped during the night. Because he spoke German Herky had become the interpreter for our compound of the POW camp and was also one of our interpreters during our long journey. The Germans had trusted him more and more as he became quite friendly and ever so cooperative and agreeable with them. Our march was delayed for over an hour until the Germans realized that Herky and his two friends had probably escaped several hours earlier.

Finally, over fifty years later on 14 December 1995 I met Herman Strietburger, our radio operator, at our Ninety-eighth Bomb Group's fiftieth reunion, along with four other of our crew who are still living. And for the first time Herky gave me the details of his escape.

At about midnight the Germans had left Herky and his two accomplices in the escape alone as they were cleaning up the kitchen where they'd boiled water for us. Polish prisoners sneaked in and gave them civilian clothes that the Polish wore; this had been previously arranged. When Herky and his two buddies were sure the Germans had gone to bed and were asleep as reported to them by the Polish prisoners, they left. Allied and German gunfire could be heard in the distance, probably only fifteen or twenty miles away. One Polish prisoner escorted them to the edge of the village and showed them the easiest way to go to reach a wooded area where they could hide until the Allies came. About two hours later Herky and his friends found this place. Herky had managed to save instant coffee and cigarettes from the Red Cross parcels. Because they were well-hidden deep in the woods, Herky felt it was safe to build a small fire to heat water for coffee. Also they planned to roast potatoes in the coals of the fire. They did this, feeling quite secure as they drank their coffee and waited for the potatoes to roast. Suddenly a bright flashlight flashed on them.

"Who is there?" shouted a voice in German. "Don't move or you will be shot!"

Two German soldiers emerged from the darkness. "Get up! Come with us immediately!"

Herky calmly spoke to them in German. "Let's talk this situation over," he answered. "We are only a few miles from the Allied lines. You have lost the war. You will be taken prisoner by the Americans, British, or Russians. It's been reported that the Russians are not taking German prisoners. They've been shooting the captured Germans.

"Here, have an American cigarette," Herky said. "We'll fix you a real cup of coffee also," he continued.

The German soldiers accepted the cigarettes and also had instant coffee. Herky, being the interpreter for our group, had managed to save coffee, soap, and cigarettes from the Red Cross parcels. He had done many favors for us POWs, and many repaid his kindness with parts of their parcels which they'd received months ago. After the Germans had finished their cigarettes and coffee, they suddenly decided to leave. Heavy Allied and German gunfire could be heard only a few miles away. This probably made their decision easier. Herky and friends were greatly relieved that they had not been caught by fanatical German soldiers who had a "Hitler mentality." After the Germans left, they put out their bonfire and quickly walked across a wide, dark farm field and into a dense wooded area about two miles away. Here they lay down in beds of dry leaves and soon fell asleep.

At the break of dawn Herky awakened and aroused his two pals. They quickly gathered their blankets and other meager belongings and moved deeper into the forest to get farther away from any roads that the advancing Allies and retreating Germans would be using. Then they settled down to wait until nightfall before moving. Herky said that time passed very slowly but that they were encouraged because the sound of battle gunfire kept coming closer.

For three more days they followed the same procedure, but then they hid in woods only about a mile from a main road that they thought the advancing Allies would probably use. Loud rumbles, almost like thunder, were heard by them, which seemed to be only a couple of miles away. Then, at about noon, Herky and his friends could make out the distant rumble of advancing tanks as well as nearby rifle fire. They anxiously awaited the oncoming Allies. Herky told the others that they'd lay low until the Allies pushed the Germans well beyond them, and then they'd contact the Allies. At this time they didn't know if the Allies were British or Americans. At about three o'clock in the afternoon they crept closer to the road where the armies were advancing. Cautiously looking through the forest, they finally recognized Allied troops. After waiting another hour or more, Herky determined that it was safe for them to make their appearance to the Allies. He and the other two escaping POWs tied what was left of their dirty white underwear on a long stick to hold up in surrendering fashion as they slowly approached the Allies. Soon Herky and his pals cautiously approached the troops as they waved their surrender flag.

"They're not Krauts, they're bloody, bloomin' Yanks!" shouted a British soldier.

Words aren't sufficient to describe the elation of Herky and his friends. They hugged and were hugged by the British soldiers. After much excited and noisy chatter, the British told them to wait until nearby advancing trucks in the rear came; then they'd get a much-deserved ride to a safe place. The passing British soldiers waved, shouted, and cheered as they recognized the liberated Yankees. About a half hour later a convoy of British trucks came. One driver stopped and told them to get aboard.

"You're lucky, the war's over for you!" exclaimed a British soldier.

"We have to get all these bloody Krauts before it's over for us. They refuse to surrender even though they know they've lost the war!" shouted another.

Herky and his comrades enjoyed their ride into a German village a few kilometers away where they were given quarters in a house that had been evacuated by the German civilians. After the British allowed them to bathe, Herky and pals were given clean British uniforms. The British also gave them bread, cheese, and a small glass of wine. Then they were told that they'd be deloused as soon as they got the delousing disinfectants. About an hour later the British had them apply de-lousing medication several times as they bathed again. Herky said it was like heaven to feel clean again; he even thought, though they were quite skinny, that they looked rather handsome in their British uniforms!

A week later, after an enjoyable time with the British, Herky and his two pals were driven by British truck about twenty miles and were turned over to American troops. To make a long experience short, Herky and his buddies got back to the States only eleven days before the rest of us liberated POWs. Were these few days of freedom worth the risks they'd taken? I think not, considering all they'd previously been through!

Meanwhile the remainder of the several thousand of us POWs were stopped at a huge internment camp, an international one, at Falengbastel, Germany. This was said to be the largest POW camp in Germany. Word circulated that there were about fifty thousand POWs here and that most were French and Russian. The French and Russians worked on farms and were now busy planting potatoes, as were prisoners of many other nationalities who had been captured by the Germans. We were surprised to see Greeks, Turks, Arabs, Africans, and even some Gypsies and others.

We were happy to see that the Germans allowed the POWs at Falengbastel to build small bonfires. Russian and French prisoners had potatoes that they had put into their pockets while planting them. Some of us had bars of soap we'd saved. Soap was almost as valuable for trading for food as American cigarettes. I traded my last bar of soap to a Russian for about a dozen pota-toes. The Germans allowed us to gather wood, dead tree limbs, from a nearby forest to use as firewood. Lou, our ball turret gun-ner, and I volunteered along with ten others to help pull a wagon to the forest to get wood. As we loaded the wagon, Lou and I fixed a large bundle especially for ourselves. About an hour later we trudged into the camp with a heavy load of wood. When we stopped the wagon, Russian prisoners attacked it and began tak-ing the wood. Because all of us who had labored and gathered the wood were Americans, we wanted to share it with just our own men. All of us grabbed sticks and tried to beat off the Russians. We fought them off furiously until our buddies over-whelmed the Russians and got most of the wood. Later as I thought about this battle it reminded me of a nature movie I had seen in which a pride of lions and many hyenas fought over a kill the lions had made. In this case the "American Lions" had won a decisive victory. The German guards had just stood close by, laughing and enjoying the engagement. Lou remarked that we'd probably have to have another war to beat the damned, mean Russians. It was rather prophetic, I later realized, as our General Patton said the same thing a few months later.

There was much excitement at Falengbastel when the rumor started that we were about to be liberated. This, plus the fact that most of us were able to trade something to the Russian and French prisoners for potatoes which we baked in the ashes of our bonfires. We felt better than we had in about two months, during which we'd gone without warm food. Our spirits, which had sunken to an extremely low level bordering on despair, were greatly uplifted. Lou, Ozzie (our roommate from Milwaukee), and I sat close to each other in the cool, damp air near our fire enjoy-ing our roasted potatoes. Ozzie broke the silence and said once again, "When I get home, I'll have Mom make fried chicken and a big skillet of fried potatoes and onions. I love fried potatoes and onions, and I can eat a whole skillet full by myself."

Lou answered, "I'd prefer a large T-bone steak and no potatoes. I'm tired of these damned potatoes!"

I agreed with Lou and replied that I'd like the T-bone steak and strawberry shortcake for dessert and also a large piece of Mom's coconut cake. Then we ate silently, but I knew we were all three thinking of home and our families. I had a clear mental picture of my family seated around our large kitchen table having Sunday dinner. We were eating fried chicken, mashed potatoes, gravy, corn on the cob, and green beans, our most common Sunday dinner. I could see dear Mom at the head of our long, rectangular table and Dad seated on her right. On Mom's left was little Raymond-he was twelve years old now. On Dad's right was Martha, my youngest sister, who was now fourteen. Next to Martha should have been Wilma, my sister who would have been twenty-five now. Dear Wilma had died at age twenty-four of a brain hemorrhage during an epileptic seizure in 1943 while I was stationed at Lowry Field, Colorado.

Lou noticed the tears streaming down my face and said softly, "What's the matter, Frank?"

"Nothing, I was just thinking about home," I replied.

Much to our dismay, chagrin, and disgust, the next morning (it was 25 April 1945) all of us American prisoners were lined up in our columns of five-we'd probably done this hundreds of times-and once again began our dismal march. At least the weather was good; the temperature was probably in the sixties, and the sun was shining. This was one of our better days, much better than the many cold, freezing days, or the ones when the spring rains were heavy. We walked about fifteen kilometers before we were once again housed in barns near a small German village. Because there were a couple of hours of daylight left we were allowed to sit outside our barn. As usual we looked around for mounds of dirt in which potatoes, turnips, etc., were buried. Soon we dug into a mound and found some potatoes which we put into our shirt bags. The two days of having roasted potatoes in Falengbastel was our first and last cooked food we had for almost two months.

Each day the German guards talked less and seemed very depressed. They knew they'd lost the war and occasionally one would say to us, "All is kaput. Der war is over," in half-German and half-English.

The next few days dragged on slowly. We continued to walk. How or why the Germans continued to fight a war that they'd obviously lost was unreasonable to us. Their supply routes, as we passed them each day, showed many wagons pulled by horses with war supplies; their only vehicles were wood-burning, steam-powered trucks. It was clear to us that we had knocked out their oil supplies, especially in Ploesti, Romania, where our crew had flown four missions from our base in Lecce, Italy.

On 1 May 1945 we had bedded down, as on most occasions, in a large barn. There must have been five hundred of us as we were so crowded. When we awakened on the morning of 2 May 1945 the sun was shining brightly and it was at least 6:30 A.M. To our surprise there were only three German guards, three older ones. They were probably in their fifties which seemed quite old to us.

"All is kaput. Der war is over!" he said quite meekly.

We were happy and somewhat bewildered at the same time. For a few minutes we just walked around the open area around the barn and farmhouse. There was no loud cheering or shouting from us. We seemed to be in a daze. Our eighty-seven-day journey had taken its toll; we were greatly relieved, but we obviously were in a state of depression brought on by so many days of deprivation that our physical and mental conditions were severely damaged.

Then about a half dozen Polish prisoners approached us and asked if we'd like some food. At least we were able to get this message from their mixture of Polish and broken English. First they directed us to a small cheese factory. Large hoops of cheese were stored in a dark, cool room. They cut us large chunks of cheese; some newly freed prisoners took huge chunks, ten pounds or more. The Polish friends then gave us bread and wine. Meanwhile the Polish men and women were chasing the German civilians out of their houses and village. Most of them had already packed their belongings and fled.

That night we had a big feast. The few remaining chickens were cleaned and dressed by the Polish people and those of us who had grown up on farms back in the USA. These German chickens and mashed potatoes with gravy were greatly appreciated by all of us.

Meanwhile the British had told us to stay in the German village until the next day because nearby Luneburg, Germany, had been the site of a large battle. The British had won, but they told us that because there were still German snipers between us and Luneburg it would be dangerous to proceed this day. So we stayed, ate dinner, and slept in good beds for the first time in many months, and many years, for some of us.

The next morning, 3 May 1945, many of our group began looking for any available means of transportation. If we didn't find any, we'd have to walk to Luneburg, which was about ten miles away. Some found bicycles, and I looked around as I heard a wood-burning truck. Lou and several others were riding in it. Lou was tossing wood into the burner to create the steam. He waved and shouted at me as they sped by. Several other friends and I decided to walk. We tossed away any of our few belongings we thought we'd no longer need.

So began the final leg of our eighty-seven-day walk which we later called "The Black Hunger March." Those of us who had survived would remember it for the rest of our lives as the worst time in our lives. At the time I'm sure we didn't realize it, but our lives had been changed forever; our personalities had changed as well as our complete outlook on life in general. This final march was a gruesome one. Because the battle had only ended the day before, there were still slain bodies, both German and British, on the ground. Some of the bodies were being removed by British soldiers. Some of the dead had rifles, pistols, and other weapons lying beside them. A few of our group stopped to pick up some of these weapons for souvenirs, but most of us wanted no part of them.

Because most of our German guards had left before we were freed, along with the fact that most of them were not mean to us, I knew of only one instance where our prisoners had taken revenge. There was one large German guard who was at least six feet seven inches tall who had been extremely cruel to many of us. He was with another group of our men when we were liberated, so I didn't observe what happened to him. But my friend Marvin Alford was with his group. "Big Stoop," as this tall German guard was called by us when he was not within hearing distance, was killed by some of our men who had been mistreated by him. Marvin witnessed his execution; he was beheaded, or perhaps I should say decapitated! To my knowledge this was the only incident of our group involving themselves with revenge against the Germans. Among us there seemed to be very little hatred toward the Germans. We were all grateful that we had survived, and thought of many of our pals who hadn't made it.

After walking through the battlefield at Luneburg we arrived at the British camp. The British had set up tents and were well organized. They had begun putting up tents for us when they'd received word of our liberation, and were prepared. We were given a warm, cheerful welcome by the British. After they served us tea and food, they let us begin our clean-up and bathing. We had worn the same clothes for eighty-seven days through snow, sleet, and rain. We were told to remove our bloody, filthy clothes. Then the British piled them in a huge mound and burned them. We took showers and then were covered with delousing medication. After a few minutes we repeated the process. Then we felt completely clean for the first time in many months. Next we were given clean underwear and complete British uniforms which included a cap. We called the cap a "tam." Some thought it was cute. The British then gave us another cup of tea and told us we could rest. Since we were very tired we soon fell asleep. When we awakened on the morning of 3 May 1945 we felt better and more rested than we had in months.

For breakfast each morning while we were with the British we had all the porridge we could eat. Finally at age twenty-two I learned that porridge, the kind that Goldilocks ate in the famous story "The Three Bears," was nothing more than oatmeal. We were given all the food we wanted, and our appetites were insatiable. But none of us became sick from overeating. Although we remained with the British for a week, none of us were impatient about leaving sooner to join our American troops; we were very content. I greatly appreciated the good-natured, quite caustic sense of humor the British displayed with us.

On 4 May 1945 while with the British at Luneburg, we learned that the war in Europe had ended. Although we did join in with the British troops with some loud cheering, jumping up and down, and hugging each other, our celebration was nothing like the loud and boisterous one that we later saw on newsreels back in the States. We obviously were still too tired, mentally and physically, from our long journey to display much enthusiasm.

On 9 May 1945 we were told that we'd be flown to Brussels, Belgium, for two days before being flown to France. The British gave us a cheerful, rousing send-off. One especially vocal British soldier shouted as we departed, "Good-bye and good luck; we do like you, you bloody, bloomin' Yanks! You did help us just a bit in winning this bloody war!"

That was the first time the word "bloody" seemed to have been used appropriately by him.

We were each given twenty dollars and were boarded on an army air force plane for the flight to Brussels. From the airport we were taken by bus to downtown Brussels.

Four of us who had managed to stay together on our eighty-seven-day journey over the German countryside—Lou, our ball turret gunner, from Pennsylvania; Floyd Vickery from Michigan; Rudy (Ozzie) Oswaldt from Milwaukee; and myself from Mississippi, were very close friends; we had been together in our room of twenty-four men back in prison camp. As we explored Brussels we found it to be a very interesting city. Because we were wearing British uniforms the local populace thought we were British troops. A few spoke to us in English.

During our two-day stay in Brussels the four of us got hair cuts, went to a movie, had our picture taken at a photomat, which showed off our British uniforms, ate a steak dinner and other meals, and had a great time in general. We even weighed ourselves again. Surprisingly I now weighed 128 pounds; I'd gained ten pounds since the British had weighed us about a week ago.

Our two-day tour of Brussels ended and we were flown to Camp Lucky Strike in France. There we joined thousands and thousands of USGI personnel. We were given army air force uniforms, but we kept our British ones. Also we were put on a rigid diet because we weren't accustomed to eating a full, regular diet; at least that's what the U.S. Army personnel thought. Although all of us tried to tell them that the British had given us all we wanted to eat, it was to no avail. The first night we found and sneaked into a food supply tent to get more food. When we proceeded to open the gallon cans I discovered that, in the dark, I'd taken a gallon of green beans, Lou had taken a gallon of green peas, and Ozzie got a gallon of tomatoes. We did eat some of each.

The only officer on our crew whom I met at Camp Lucky Strike was Bob Moore, our navigator. We were very happy to meet again after our long ordeal as POWs. We had last seen each other as we were being interrogated in the jail in Budapest, Hungary, on 28 June 1944, almost eleven months earlier.

On 12 June 1945 Bob and I were called to a meeting with two American officers, a major and a captain. They were quite polite but soon began to quiz us about what had happened to Nick Kish, our nose gunner. Bob and I together told them the following accounts:

As our plane was going down in flames and the bomb bay was on fire I fastened on my chest-pack parachute and went to the nose of our plane to jump from the nose-wheel door. Bob was standing there with Nick Kish and Vern Huff, our bombardier. Bob told me to jump, and I did. Later when we were captured Bob told me, as he now told the major and captain, that Nick said he didn't have a parachute. Bob told him to go to the flight deck to get the extra one we always had there. But he said that Nick just stood frozen in his tracks. Then Bob told him to hang onto his harness and they'd jump together. When Nick shook his head indicating "no," Bob jumped. Because it was my duty to stand by and see that each man had a chute as he boarded our plane, I was asked if Nick had his parachute as he had boarded. I was positive that he had one. After a half hour or so we convinced these officers that we were telling the truth. We were very sad that Nick was killed when our plane crashed and exploded.

On 10 June 1945 approximately a thousand of us boarded the Marine Robin, a converted cargo ship, for our greatly anticipated trip home. Although we were very crowded on the ship and had triple-deck canvas-cot-type bunks–and mine was in the middle–we were much more comfortable than we'd been accustomed to in prison camp. I was fortunate enough to have my friends, Floyd Vickery from Michigan, Marvin Alford from my hometown, and G. W. Mize from Jackson, Mississippi, with me aboard the ship. G. W. had joined our march for about three weeks or so before we were liberated near Luneburg, Germany. G. W. had been captured in the Battle of the Bulge.

Our trip to New York took six days and seven nights and was quite uneventful. We lounged on the deck, played cards and talked. Each day was much the same.

When the Statue of Liberty was in view in the distance, loud, happy, thunderous roars of cheer and shrill whistling filled the air. The cheering continued until we slowly pulled into the harbor. Many people were standing and waving as we approached land. Some were waiting to greet their loved ones.

There was no one waiting for me and my three close friends. We had been allowed to send a telegram from France to tell our families we were safe and that we'd be home before the end of June. Also we were all given a sixty-day furlough. Marvin, G. W., and I took a train headed for Jackson, Mississippi. Floyd Vickery took one headed for Detroit, Michigan, which was near his home in Walled Lake, Michigan. Before we boarded the train in New York, G. W. had time to call his parents. He was relieved to learn that all of them were well. Marvin and I couldn't call home because we lived in the country and no one close by had phones. We had been allowed to send the telegram stating that we'd be home by the end of June.

When our train stopped in Louisville, Kentucky, for about twenty minutes, I located a pay phone and called my Aunt Burtie who lived in New Albany, Indiana, located just across the Ohio River from Louisville, Kentucky. I was greatly relieved to hear that all in my family were living and well, because it had been almost a year since I'd heard from them. But I was saddened to find out that my Uncle Yuba, Dad's brother, had died a few months earlier and Aunt Burtie was alone.

At about 7 P.M. the next night our train pulled into Jackson, Mississippi. G. W. Mize's father and mother met him at the train station. After they'd embraced G. W. numerous times while laughing and crying, they hugged Marvin and me. It really felt good to have caring adults hugging us. Then Mr. and Mrs. Mize offered to drive Marvin and me home, but we told them we'd have our relatives come for us because it would be about a thirty-mile round-trip for them.

After we said farewell to G. W. and his parents, Marvin and I walked a short distance to a restaurant. Marvin called a cousin who said he'd pick us up in about an hour. So we decided to have a steak dinner; in 1945 it only cost one dollar and fifty cents. We were surprised that we knew our waitress, Elsie Hemphill. I had graduated from high school with her sister, Audrey.

A few minutes after we had been served, Elsie said, "Marvin, I was so sorry to hear about your brother passing away."

Marvin stopped eating–that was the end of his meal. His brother had died about two months earlier; he was only in his thirties. Although my appetite wasn't too good at this point, I managed to finish my meal. We didn't talk much while we waited for our friend to meet us. Another of Marvin's cousins, Bobby Jo Laird, also came to meet us. Bobby Jo had graduated from Florence High with my younger sister, Ruth, and they were friends. She told me that Ruth was the valedictorian of the class of 1945, that she had a lead role in their senior play, and also that she had been voted Florence High's most intelligent girl in their student "Who's Who" contest. Bobby Jo and I talked all the way home; she told us the local news of the past year.

At about midnight we pulled into the lane leading to our farmhouse. At the large gate at the end of the lane I got out of the car, thanked Marvin and his cousins, and walked about a hundred yards to our home. It was a very dark June night, but I could faintly see the road. Suddenly a noise in the brush beside the road startled me. Then my dog, Toby, was jumping all over me. Toby, a good watchdog, had not forgotten me; he didn't even bark!

As I approached our house I noticed a light inside, and I could see Dad sitting by the living room table; he was reading by lamplight. I tapped softly on the door so I wouldn't startle him. After Dad and I embraced and talked a few minutes, I softly walked into Mom's bedroom where she was asleep.

"Mom, it's me, Frank," I said as I gently patted her back.

"Oh!" Mom screamed as she sat up in bed.

Then she immediately calmed down as she realized I was really home. She said that she had thought she was having a bad dream.

The well-known author Thomas Wolfe has a book title that states You Can't Go Home Again. I disagree. As long as I have one close, living relative, I shall go home again, because it's among the most wonderful experiences I've ever had!

Biographical sketches of the crew of the American Maid.

1st Lt. David Himes, Pilot
1st Lt. Paul Stillions, Copilot
1st Lt. Robert Moore, Navigator
1st Lt. Vernon Huff, Bombardier
TSgt. Herman Strietburger, Radio Operator
TSgt. Louis Staudenemier, Ball Turret Gunner
TSgt. Ellis Covan, Tail Gunner
TSgt. Nicholas Kish, Nose Gunner
TSgt. Eugene Bailey, Waist Gunner
TSgt. James Catron, Waist Gunner
TSgt. Frank Farnsley, Top Turret Gunner

1st Lt. David Himes, Pilot

David Himes, 1972

In 1945 David married Merle Keeron, a flight nurse in the U.S. Army. They had two sons, David Jr. and John. Both followed in their father's footsteps–David Jr., who has now retired from the U.S. Air Force, and John, who is in the U.S. Army and expects to retire in two years.

From 1945 to 1948 David was assigned to flight-testing at Tinker AFB. In 1948 David spent eight months on the Berlin airlift. He was assigned to Eglin AFB in Research and Development. At this time he began to fly jet aircraft. He was one of the four officers who spent eighteen months at Boeing Aircraft in Wichita, Kansas, helping to develop and test the B-47 for the air force.

Until his retirement as a colonel in 1972, David was assigned to different B-47 wings as an instructor pilot and logistics commander. He was also assigned to the B-52 pilot training and the fighter wing at V Bon, Thailand, as logistic commander. David also spent one year at the Pentagon. He retired at Andrews AFB in 1972 as deputy wing commander.

Like the rest of his crew, David appreciated his freedom more as a result of his POW experiences.

David died suddenly of a heart attack in 1988.

1st Lt. Paul Stillions, Copilot

Paul Stillions with his wife, Jo, 1995

Paul was born and grew up in Charleston, Illinois. He and his wife, Jo, have two children and four grandsons. He did his B-24 training at Almagordo, New Mexico, and in Charleston, South Carolina.

Paul served with the 516th Troop Carrier Group Reserve in Memphis, Tennessee, from 1945 to 1951. From 1951 to 1954 he served with the 173d. Air Transport Group at Brookley Field, Alabama, as a C-54 pilot. He also served as a liaison officer to the Caribbean Air Command at Albrook AFB in Panama.

From 1954 to 1964 Paul was in the Active Reserve-Retired Reserve. At the time he retired from the U.S. Air Force in 1982, Paul was a lieutenant colonel.

After his military service ended in 1964, Paul worked for Sears Roebuck & Company as a merchandise control buyer. He was a field supervisor and in charge of catalogue sales in four states. He then worked for Holiday Inn, Inc., as Western Territory Manager. Several years before he retired, Paul was a private pilot for Holiday Inn. After retirement he was the commander of the mid-south chapter of the American Ex-Prisoner of War Organization.

Paul stated that his POW experiences made him a better person who appreciated and enjoyed life and freedom much more because of them, and that he considers these experiences very beneficial.

1st Lt. Robert Moore, Navigator

Bob Moore was our capable navigator who remained in the air force after the war. Then he went through pilot training. He flew as a pilot for several years and then attended maintenance school. Bob retired in 1963 and went to electronics school. After he completed this training, he worked in his hometown as a TV and radio repairman.

Bob and his wife, Myrtle, have four children and nine

Robert Moore with his wife, Myrtle, 1995

grandchildren. Bob said that he regards his POW experiences as a valuable lesson in self-sufficiency. However he also said, "Needless to say, I do not recommend POW experiences to anyone!"

TSgt. Herman Strietburger, Radio Operator

left to right: Herman Strietburger, his sister and his wife, 1995

Herk worked for the Rheingold Brewery in Brooklyn, New York, for thirty-one years. He serviced retail accounts in New York City for twenty years. Also he was the company's manager for Maine, New Hampshire, and Vermont for eleven years. Herk's last ten working years were spent in sales management for a master distributor covering the state of New Hampshire. In 1986 he retired.

Herk and his wife, Jackie, were married in 1949. Twin daughters, Jan and Kim, were followed by two boys, Guy and Ross. All are married. Herk stated that he and Jackie found one of the greatest benefits of retirement to be their six grandchildren: Guy, Jeffery, Jessica, Kyle, Lindsay, Johnny, and Julie. They are their treasures.

Herk says that he is most grateful for having survived his POW experience, and that it taught him lessons he could never have learned from a book. He further states that it sharpened his wits and that he developed lasting friendships to this day. He firmly believes that the discipline his parents and teachers taught him resulted in his survival. Herk says that imprisonment made him more appreciative of all life has to offer and of the freedom he enjoys as an American.

TSgt. Louis Staudenemier, Ball Turret Gunner

Louis was born in Ashland, Pennsylvania, into a family of eleven children–nine boys and two girls. His father died when he

was eight years old. Although his mother never remarried she managed to work and keep the family together. Lou and all of his brothers and sisters graduated from Ashland High School.

Lou has a dry, witty sense of humor; he was well-liked by his crew members.

Louis Staudenemier with his wife, Winifred, 1995

After the war Lou was employed by Prudential Insurance Company. After many sales seminars, he took an agency with Prudential. He married Winifred Murphy in 1958. He and Winifred have four children all of whom obtained college degrees. They are Joseph, Paul, Caroline, and Marianne.

After thirty-five years with Prudential, Lou retired.

Lou said that life in prison camp made him aware of the imperfections in himself and other people. Also he stated that learning to live so closely with people from all walks of life made him a more tolerant person. He said that now he appreciates the simpler things of life, like a walk in the woods, gardening, and playing golf. Occasionally he says he dreams of what happened so long ago, but with the coming of daylight the dreams are dismissed.

Lou gave his children this advice: Never make hard decisions in the dark of night because problems always look different in daylight.

TSgt. Ellis Covan, Tail Gunner

Ellis was our six-foot-tall gunner from Alabama. A well-built young man, he was a fun-loving, carefree person who fully enjoyed life.

For about ten years we corresponded. In 1955, from the last letter I received from him, Ellis was working at an aircraft factory in California. He had been mugged, robbed, and seriously injured in Los Angeles. After several months in the hospital he recovered. Because he wrote to me about six times a year and I never heard from him again, being unable to contact him by phone, I feel that he may have passed away. I also tried to locate relatives in Alabama, but I was unsuccessful.

TSgt. Nicholas Kish, Nose Gunner

Nick was from Indiana, Pennsylvania, where he had attended Indiana College. A good athlete, he played on the baseball and football teams. He lived with his older brother and sister-in-law who were like parents to him. His sister-in-law told me that all they were ever told of Nick's fate was that he was missing in action, and after a year the U.S. Army Air Force sent them a telegram stating that he had been killed in action. A few months ago I told Nick's brother the details of Nick's death. Nick's sister-in-law told me Nick's remains were returned in 1950, and that he was interred in Indiana, Pennsylvania.

TSgt. Eugene Bailey, Waist Gunner

Gene was a short, friendly young man from Savannah, Georgia. He spoke with the southeastern Georgia accent. Although we got to know Gene well in POW camp, we have been unable to locate him or any of his relatives. So we have assumed that he is probably deceased.

TSgt. James Catron, Waist Gunner

(James finished his fiftieth mission the day before our plane was shot down.)

In 1942 Jim and Helen were married. They have no children but lost a baby in 1945. Jim worked for Hercules Powder Co. and was drafted into the Army Air Corps in 1943. After being discharged in 1945 he went to the Cincinnati College of Embalming for one year. Jim went to work for the Williams Funeral Home of Chilhowie, Inc., in 1946. He has been with this firm continuously since then and is still working part-time.

Jim says his combat experience made him realize that he is very lucky to be alive. He also states that it made him realize that he is not immortal, and that he is thankful for all the friends he has made over the years.

TSgt. Frank Farnsley, Top Turret Gunner

Frank came from a family of nine children, four boys and five girls, and lived on a farm near Jackson, Mississippi. He graduated from high school in 1940 and then attended business college in Jackson. In March of 1943 Frank went into the Army Air Corps and was discharged on his birthday, 17 October 1945.

Frank Farnsley with his wife, Clara, 1995

In 1958, Frank married Clara Rains from Nebraska and Colorado Springs, Colorado. He and Clara both taught in the Hammond, Indiana public schools for twenty-four years before retiring. Clara was a first grade teacher and Frank taught all grades, second through eighth, as well as high school English. He was also a principal and an assistant principal.

Frank and Clara have two children–Kevin, who is an electrical engineer, and Rebecca, who is a nurse. They have five grandchildren. Kevin's children are Nicole, Bradley, and Mitchel. Julie and Brian are Becky's children.

Frank says that his POW experiences, although very difficult to endure, made him a better person. He feels it made him a more thoughtful person who better understands and cares about other people's suffering. And Frank says he knows he appreciates the more simple and mundane aspects of life as well as the true meaning of freedom.